What people are saying about

The Medicine Clothes that Look at the People

The tales of original peoples guide us back to richness and authenticity, to a relationship with heart and Earth, and to what makes us whole. This book, a precious gift from the Pacific Northwest Samish people, is transmitted masterfully by Whis. Stem.Men.Knee, healer and spiritual leader who carries the Si.Si. Wiss "Sacred Breath, Sacred Life" teachings of his people. As he picks up story threads woven by the grandparents of long ago, Johnny Moses breathes to life treasured, ancient wisdom that can help us breathe sacredness back to modern times.

Llyn Cedar Roberts, MA, award-winning author and founder of the Olympic Mountain EarthWisdom Circle

The Medicine Clothes That Look At The People unfolds the magic that lives in First Peoples' tales. Johnny Moses whose traditional name means "Walking Medicine Robe" lives and breathes the power of these stories, after learning them through many nights, days and years, from the elders. Now he holds them in his bones. While you read, allow yourself to fall more deeply into your wise heart. The heart knows that stories have power. The power to heal us, the power to strengthen us, the power to help us listen to our soul's voice, and the power to weave our human family back together.

Evelyn C. Rysdyk, author of *Th· ᴺ··· ·········· · · ·t Walking*. Co-author with Nepales *The Nepalese Shamanic Path*

Johnny Moses is a legendary st⊂ ⸱ planet when so many people have lost their way, Johnny Moses shares the traditional stories that create a road map leading us back home to ourselves, and to the Earth. I was so touched by this story, *The Medicine Clothes That Look at the People*.

Sandra Ingerman, **MA**, author of Walking in Light and The Book of Ceremony

The Medicine Clothes that Look at the People

Ancient Pacific Northwest Samish Tale

The Medicine Clothes that Look at the People

Ancient Pacific Northwest Samish Tale

Told by Johnny Moses

(Whis.Stem.Men.Knee)

**MOON
BOOKS**

Winchester, UK
Washington, USA

JOHN HUNT PUBLISHING

First published by Moon Books, 2020
Moon Books is an imprint of John Hunt Publishing Ltd., No. 3 East Street, Alresford
Hampshire SO24 9EE, UK
office@jhpbooks.net
www.johnhuntpublishing.com
www.moon-books.net

For distributor details and how to order please visit the 'Ordering' section on our website.

Text copyright: Johnny Moses 2019

ISBN: 978 1 78904 395 2
978 1 78904 396 9 (ebook)
Library of Congress Control Number: 2019941757

A CIP catalogue record for this book is available from the British Library.

Design: Stuart Davies

UK: Printed and bound by CPI Group (UK) Ltd, Croydon, CR0 4YY
US: Printed and bound by Thomson-Shore, 7300 West Joy Road, Dexter, MI 48130

We operate a distinctive and ethical publishing philosophy in all areas of our business, from our global network of authors to production and worldwide distribution.

Contents

SPONSOR'S NOTE

In July 2018, Llyn Cedar Roberts, independent filmmaker, Mitch Mattraw, and Rob Murphy of the *Olympic Mountain EarthWisdom Circle* (OMEC) were invited by Bill Cote, host of the Red Cedar Circle spiritual gathering in Port Townsend, WA, to an event featuring Johnny Moses, a Tulalip Native American traditional storyteller. Johnny's traditional name *Whis.Stem.Men.Knee* translates as "Walking Medicine Robe". He carries the *Si.Si.Wiss* - "Sacred Breath, Sacred Life" teachings of his people.

Having supported book projects from diverse parts of the world, OMEC – dedicated to encouraging a scared and responsible relationship with the Earth and to preserving ancient wisdom ways – through this publication supports the indigenous wisdom of the Pacific Northwest, where the organization was founded.

We are delighted to present *"The Medicine Clothes that Look at the People"*, a Samish story transcribed from a live event with master storyteller, Johnny Moses. In Johnny's tradition, those listening to the traditional stories are invited to respond in refrain to his passages, with the words: *Eee Nae Weyth* "I am listening." As you read this book, we invite you to imagine sitting in circle with Johnny Moses as he takes you on this sacred journey.

Rob Murphy
Vice-President, Olympic Mountain EarthWisdom Circle
Olympic Peninsula, Washington State, January 2019.

FIRST NIGHT

This story that I want to start out with. This story is a very old story. This is the story of a medicine woman who wears medicine clothes, very beautiful clothes. She goes visiting the medicine people and as she is visiting, she wears different kinds of clothes to visit the different ones who she is going to help or where she is going to get help from. And the name of this story it is from the Samish people and it is the story called

The Clothes That Look at the People

Translated; the clothes, or the medicine clothes that look at the people

If you are listening to this story you can say, Eee Nae Weyth
Eee Nae Weyth
Eee nee nah ah
Whay se ne
Teeee tee
Quan se quan
Snay eet
Eee nee nah ah means soul clothes of the east
Whay se ne means soul clothes of the north
Teeee tee means soul clothes of the west
Quan se quan means soul clothes of the south
Snay eet means soul clothes of our dreams; dreams of the dream
 world
Eee Nae Weyth
There was this beautiful lady who was very, very old
She must have been 100 years old
And she was so beautiful in the way she would walk
And in the way she would speak to the people
And the way she would touch the people with the feelings

1

Eee Nae Weyth
Elay whose nie ae
Queese lee eenee aye
Queese neee
Kose nie eee
Shnan thee ton naye
Schlee a nee

Translation:
Eee Nae Weyth
And she journeyed in a canoe
In this beautiful canoe that was white
It was a white canoe
And as she traveled in this white canoe
She traveled from her island, Lopez Island
All the way to Orcas Island
To the north side of Orcas Island
Eee Nae Weyth
Ne thee la quitues
Swee laslee ta suituess
Stee une sa nae han snae tae ka
Whee nae eeeith

Translation:
Eee Nae Weyth
She stepped on the beach
And when her feet touched the sand
The feet began to cry and the feet said
"Whit sta aye aye neah nae
"Hoa sa he hay aye"
First line means the tears are traveling down into the Earth from my
soul. Second line means the tears are traveling back up from the
Earth into the bottom of my feet strengthening my walk.
Eee Nae Weyth

That a person's feelings were buried under the sand
A person that was standing here
Their clothes were buried here
Eee Nae Weyth
So, she sang
And as she sang she called the power to inhale the clothes that
    were buried within the sand
And as she sang this song
It came up and she wore these clothes
And the clothes were a mixture of feelings
The clothes were very beautiful
They were in the colors of red, purple, blue, green, and black
    dots all over this dress--it was a dress
And the clothes said, "I am the feeling of pain as it laughs."
Eee Nae Weyth
And she wore this dress
And the dress possessed her
And it made her go to this house
This house where she was going to visit
She did not know these people
Eee Nae Weyth
And as she entered the house there
She began to sing again,
"Nee loffa nee
"Nish kon tow na
"Hey e yah jey e yah hay e fee
"Nuuh hey e yah hey e yah ne."
First two lines mean the song of pain traveling from my clothes.
The last two lines mean the voice of the song of pain singing to all.
The clothes of life and change.
Eee Nae Weyth
And she could feel the pain coming out of her mouth
And it felt like she wanted to laugh
And the pain was so strong

As it was coming out of her mouth
It entered the lady who she was going to visit
Eee Nae Weyth
And there the lady began to cry
A memory was returned to her
And she thanked this old woman that was beautiful
"Thank you my dear one for sending that power into me
"The pain and laughter
"As it entered my mind it opened a doorway
"A memory was returned to me
"And it will save my life."
Eee Nae Weyth
And there she knew that her work was done
And she took off this beautiful dress and she said,
"Lee soo nao teu ay
"Lay thum sthil way thum
"Swae nae aye ay."
Lee soo nao teu ay means the knowledge from inside my clothes.
Lay thum sthil way means the knowledge from the universe lives inside
my clothes
Swae nae aye ay means the knowledge outside my clothes lives in my
mind
Eee Nae Weyth
"I will turn this dress inside out now and you will wear it as
yours
"So you understand the feelings of the dress."
Eee Nae Weyth
And she continued
And she returned to the canoe
And the white canoe said,
"Ooo Nah
"Oh na heeee
"Oh na heeee
"Oh na a eee

4

"Oh na ha see
"Ha see oh na."
Ooo Nah name of water spirit just under the canoe.
Oh na heeee name of spirit of white foam sung twice for daylight and
*   night.*
Oh na a eee soul of day and night of the water.
Oh na ha see guardian spirit that watches the bottom of the canoe.
Ha see oh na name of the water spirits, the traveling road for the water.
Eee Nae Weyth
It said, "We will travel
"We will travel to the mainland
"We will travel
"And we will travel to what is now known as See aye molth, or
    Blaine, Washington
"This place called Ushoosh quan quan."
Eee Nae Weyth
Ushoosh quan quan
Ushoosh quan quan
Which literally means the clams with big mouths.
Eee Nae Weyth
The clams with big mouths
The clams with big mouths
And big tongues, too
Eee Nae Weyth
And they traveled to this village that was called the clams with
    big mouths and big tongues, too
And there as she traveled a strange feeling came over her
This beautiful old lady
The wind as it was coming to her
The wind of the south
It touched her back
Hitting her back
And her hair started blowing forward
Her beautiful long silver hair

Silver white hair
It started blowing, hitting the water, splashing
It was like her hair was like canoe paddles, paddling the canoe
Like her hair was dancing on top of the water
Eee Nae Weyth
And the south wind it carried another lost clothes
Clothes that belonged to someone who had drowned in the ocean
Clothes that belonged to a whaler
A woman whaler
Who was from way up north
She was from Nuu-chah-nulth people
The Nootka people
She was from A Ketl Talth
There she was, lost, floating
That's the only way she could travel in the ocean
Through the south wind and nobody could hear her
Eee Nae Weyth
But the power of this old lady was strong
And she was like a magnet to lost clothes
And the clothes touched her body
And she wore these clothes of the whaler
Eee Nae Weyth
And these clothes they were beautiful
They were black, shiny black
Crystal dots all around
And the name of these clothes was Whoo EE Nai, Whoo EE Nai
It was called strength but fear
Strength but fear
The kind of strength when you are throwing arrow or harpoon
Or strength when you are lifting a boulder
Or when you are saving someone from falling into the fire and
    you feel fear in your heart
Eee Nae Weyth
And she wore these clothes

And there when she landed in the village with the clams with
    big mouths and big tongues, too
Eee Nae Weyth
She was drawn out of the canoe
And there she was drawn into this house
People were singing in the house
It must have been wintertime
They were dancing
Eee Nae Weyth
And this man
After he was done dancing his power
Fee nee nee
Too lee nee Quee
Tel lee ee ee
First line is the name of the seaweed power.
Second line means the seaweed is dancing on the water.
Eee Nae Weyth
His power was seaweed
That was his power, seaweed
He was dancing,
But something was missing
What was missing was the feelings and thoughts of his wife
That once was this whaler
The one from Nuu-chah-nulth people
Eee Nae Weyth
That he was the one that was holding onto her
Parts of her soul
Wouldn't let her go
Eee Nae Weyth
And there the old woman
The beautiful old woman
She began to sing her spirit song
Her spirit song was, whe kang stee, nothingness
Eee Nae Weyth

At the time she sang everybody went blank and knew nothing
Eee Nae Weyth
As this happened she went over to the man
And she sang again
And this power came out of her mouth
That was the whaler
And it entered this man
And he wore the clothes of his wife
Eee Nae Weyth
There the soul was returned to her in the clothes
And she was able to escape
And she came out of his mouth
And he began to sing his sea weed song again
Eee Nae Weyth
And as he was singing
As he was dancing
He could see the whaler singing to him
Was very happy in his heart
Eee Nae Weyth
And the old woman
Her work was done there
She continued traveling
Eee Nae Weyth
She got to the white canoe
And the white canoe began to sing again
Eee Nae Weyth
"Whee eee ya
"Whee eee ya
"Oyya quia neeah
"Whe nah new."
Translates the following lines.
Eee Nae Weyth
The canoe was literally saying,
"I will go backwards

"When you forget about me

"I will go backwards and you will forget who you are

"We will go backwards

"To remember who we are."

Eee Nae Weyth

Leesh ka whu toop ee stee ka net

*Leesh ka whu means that the knowledge of the past, the present and the
future are living in the canoe.*

Toop ee stee ka net means the canoe is the mind of the body and
spirit.

There she traveled in her canoe

There she started traveling further north

Lay tees a tooth

The mind and spirit are traveling.

A place called Chwassen or Twassan

And they went to Chwassen or Tsawwassen

The village of

Whilth kam ah ken

Name means where the people arrive, the people welcome them.

And whilth kam ah ken is near where the ferry lands today

Not too far from there

There she was called there

And the canoe said to her,

"We must go there."

Eee Nae Weyth

And the spirit of there said,

"We must go there."

Eee Nae Weyth

And the spirit of go said,

"We must go there."

Eee Nae Weyth

And the spirit of go and there agreed that we would go there

Eee Nae Weyth

That's what it says in the story

Even in the story the words agree with one another
Eee Nae Weyth
As they traveled through the waters
They would only travel through the water trails that knew them
Eee Nae Weyth
There as they traveled
She heard a beautiful song
Of a beautiful spirit
Coming out of the whirlpool
Eee Nae Weyth
And the song went like this
"Nee nee wael nah
"Ho tan nee wan neelth."
First line is the names of different kinds of whirlpools. Second line is
the underworld whirlpool name.
The spirit was a very beautiful spirit
Le lee elth katelth ka ton
Name of that spirit.
It was a spirit of a lady who cried many years ago
Who cried because she felt lost
She felt lost even though she had a family
She felt lost
Eee Nae Weyth
And the thought of lost felt pity for her and captured her in the
    word of lost
Eee Nae Weyth
And this thought of lost fell in love with this spirit and had pity
    for her because she felt so lost
Eee Nae Weyth
So the word lost swallowed her and she was lost
Eee Nae Weyth
So the song that this old woman was hearing was the voice of
    lost
Eee Nae Weyth

She wore the clothes of lost
And the clothes could change into many beautiful colors
Eee Nae Weyth
And became the color of her skin
Eee Nae Weyth
And as she wore these clothes of lost
She began to sing her song
"Eee nee, neh e quee
"Whoolin say la nee e neh
"He lah wah sah neh weh
"Quee e e nan san nah."
Whoolin, names of spirits of lost.
Means all the spirits of lost are lost.
The word can be used to curse sickness, material things, etc.
He lah wah is spirit that knows it is lost
Sah neh weh is spirit that does not know it is lost
Quee e e is sound of a spirit. We do not know what spirit because it is lost.
Nah san nah is a lost universe that knows everything that is lost, also the word for when we take a sickness off a person and throw that sickness. This word is only used in the epic singing. These words are only used in epics or healing ceremonies. If they are used outside of this context, it is black shamanism. This is why certain families, or the older people would choose certain ones to sing these songs, because if someone who was spacey sang the lost song they would get more lost. So an older person would choose someone appropriate for different songs. Different parts of the epics.
Eee Nae Weyth
She says, "Oh where are you my dear one?
"Where are you?
"I can hear your voice
"Let me know where you are in the body of lost."
Eee Nae Weyth
There she continued in her canoe being lost in the ocean

11

Going in circles
Going in different directions
Trying to search for this soul
Eee Nae Weyth
Finally they landed near the village in Twassan country
And there she was called to this house
Eee Nae Weyth
A voice said,
"Ee nae nae weyth
"Ee nae nae weyth
"Queein nell nae
"Quin lae nae
"Quail nae nae."
First line means waiting for a long time.
Third line means time has told us it is worth waiting.
Eee Nae Weyth
And the voice said,
"Tee kawae see ka na tith."
We have been waiting a long time.
Eee Nae Weyth
And there it was a young man
And this you man looked very lonely
And she took his clothes off, of lost
And she sang over them
And she put them on him
Eee Nae Weyth
And there
Qu tees kw tal neelth
Name of a place this other power lives, like another dimension; another
time.
Qu tees means thirty lifetimes. So it is like thirty lifetimes away where
the power lives.
It was the other part of him
Kwa sees qua tee kwalt

*Means that on the other side of where you are traveling there is another
form, a body, tree, plant, anything that you can live in that form.*
Eee Nae Weyth
And this lost
The spirit of lost
It came out of the man's mouth and it said,
"Na Thae."
It is empty, the lost is empty
EMPTY
Eee Nae Weyth
And it was empty now
It had no more soul to live in its body
And it returned to the universe
Eee Nae Weyth
Her work was done now in this house
And she continued to go back to the white canoe
Eee Nae Weyth
Quee Nee
Quee lee nee eeee
The white canoe's knowledge is surrounding her.
Eee Nae Weyth
There she sang again
And she listened to what the white canoe was going to tell her
Eee Nae Weyth
And the white canoe said,
"Nae naeng na han na
"Whey nae nae a nah
"Nu sena whesna
"What ten ning
"Weth thley whleth sen."
*Nae naeng na han na means another name of how to wear knowledge, a
name of a power that will show you how to wear knowledge.*
Whey nae nae a nah is the name of an ancestor, a woman's name.
What ten ning is her grandmother who also had the white canoe power.

Weth thley whleth sen is the name of her great, great grandmother.
Eee Nae Weyth
And the white canoe said to her,
"As we travel we must carry our thoughts with us."
Eee Nae Weyth
"And as the thoughts travel the thoughts carry us with them."
Eee Nae Weyth
"As we travel we agree to carry the thoughts with us."
Eee Nae Weyth
"As the agreement travels
"Agreement agrees to carry us and the thoughts with us."
Eee Nae Weyth
That is what it says in the story literally
That all the thoughts must agree so that we will not get lost
Eee Nae Weyth
Nee lem shwee slee whit tem naa
Nee lem shwee means the spirit of the canoe that travels from
    this world to many worlds/dimensions.
Slee whit tem naa means they travel back to my body.
And she asked the canoe,
"What village we will go to next?
"When will we arrive?"
And the canoe always would answer,
"Whae na Whoa."
Daylight in this world and the other world
Or would answer,
"Tam ha."
Nighttime in this world and the other world.
Would answer,
"Day time."
"Night time."
Eee Nae Weyth
And there at that time
Whee ka suit ta thulthen

14

Tu whee see see kulken
Translates the lines that follow.
Eee Nae Weyth
The canoe would talk to her
And a vision would come before her
And it would show her exactly the time they would be there
Eee Nae Weyth
Because the spirit of time would tell her in the vision when she
    would be there
Eee Nae Weyth
And because the vision would agree to talk to time
And time would tell vision when she would be there
Eee Nae Weyth
And there would agree with vision and time
When she would be there
Eee Nae Weyth
And then of course she would have to agree to be there
Eee Nae Weyth
Nee la qua wha neee ta quee
Nee la qua means agreement.
Wha neee ta quee means of course I agree.
In the olden days people knew their every thought
Eee Nae Weyth
Because their every thought knew them
Eee Nae Weyth
Nae whey lay lem stee sus
Translates words that follow.
In the story it says the old people used to raise their young
By telling them,
"Always agree with your thoughts
"Make friends with them."
Eee Nae Weyth
"Always forgive your thoughts
"Make friends with them."

Eee Nae Weyth

Nee lem ha leese

Feeling of different thoughts.

Their feelings were different then

When a person would get an angry thought, a sad thought, a
 shameful thought they would always say,

"We a nah lay que ase tae."

All the thoughts of the Earth.

They would tell their shame thought,

"I forgive you shame thought

"I forgive you shame thought, we are good friends."

Eee Nae Weyth

And they would say, "I know you have forgiven me

"And I accept the forgiveness

"Because I know you are a shame thought or you would not say
 that."

Eee Nae Weyth

If they had an angry thought they would tell the angry thought,

"I have forgiven you angry thought

"I know you have forgiven me

"I know you can't say that."

Eee Nae Weyth

And they would say the same thing with a very sad thought

All the different thoughts

They would forgive all the thoughts

Even though the thoughts couldn't say it

Eee Nae Weyth

Na hay lay wae tae

Way tae say

Et tu sa ha lay nae se

Ka sa na la na sa na thlen na

*First two lines are powers, doctoring words to put life force into a
 person.*

Second two lines are a chant: it means doctoring over the life force you are going to step on, usually your legs and feet and hands and arms.

These words are names for life force for parts of the body, hands, legs, arms, feet.

Eee Nae Weyth

And this doctoring woman

Ne steelth koo ka lonath

Quils silth sis thilth

Names of songs of the beauty; to create more beauty.

Ne steelth is life force from a flower. Any kind of flower.

Koo ka is life force of the star, any star, any shiny thing.

Quils silth means taking life force from any beautiful clothes, drums, baskets; also a name for a beautiful potlatch. When you see a beautiful potlatch and take the beauty from it.

Sis thilth is taking the beauty in our body and putting it in anything living and taking it back to our body again.

This doctoring woman that was very old and very beautiful

Eee Nae Weyth

Nee whoa tells

A dream world, not your dream world, but a dream world where anyone can go.

In the dream world she used her thoughts to create beautiful songs

Eee Nae Weyth

Because her songs only loved beautiful thoughts

Eee Nae Weyth

And her thoughts loved to sing beautiful songs

Eee Nae Weyth

That her thoughts and songs agreed they were beautiful

Eee Nae Weyth

When she would doctor with songs

When she would lay a hand on someone

When it was a really sad song

She knew the person was going to die

Eee Nae Weyth

And so she would comfort them and sing songs of comfort

And she'd say to them,

"Nee nee lum wquom

"Sun ten nae la."

Name of the power.

Nee nee lum and lum wquom are powers of comfort.

Sun ten nae ta, sun ten is a loving doctoring spirit power.

"I know you are going to die

"But you are going to die comfortable."

Eee Nae Weyth

"When you leave you will be surrounded by beautiful songs."

Eee Nae Weyth

This is the way she doctored

And in the olden days they prophesied

The people would forget how beautiful they were

Because they did not wrap themselves in beautiful songs

Eee Nae Weyth

Nee thlee nee lee tweathoo

Hoon sun ne

Hain nain tain sain

Powers you call on to prophecy or tell the future, to come back and tell
you what you need to know.

Hain nain tain sain is power of death in the future that can come back.

Hoon sun ne is power of life in the future.

They always call all of these powers at the same time. If you call only
one you can cause death.

Eee Nae Weyth

And she travelled back to Orcas Island from the northern country

And she travelled to the place now known as Madrona Point

Qua kae saelth

Name of the place she traveled to where the ferry now lands on Orcas
Island. There is a lady buried there. That is her name.

And there she heard another song

Eee Nae Weyth
And the song said,
"Wee whoo eee
"Whoo un nah
"Tee sielt ten nen
"Nee ahn na
"Queee."
Translated in words that follow.
The song said, "When I believe I feel all the secret sad feelings of my
    friends and relatives."
Eee Nae Weyth
She prayed and she put her hands up
And she asked her hands,
"I cannot see, hands
"Hands see for me."
Eee Nae Weyth
And the hands would say,
"Ah nah qu nan nalth nee."
Ah nah means the hands are speaking.
Qu nan nalth nee means the energies, the other energies are speaking
    to the hands.
She cannot see
Her eyeballs cannot see
We have better eyesight, hands
Eee Nae Weyth
Nee kalth ah nee
A nee eee eee
Whooo Teethl
These words literally mean traveling through the eyes not through
    anything else. A nee eee eee means the feeling of the eyes.
And they seen this soul
And they put the hands together
The eyes talked to one another
And they carried what they had seen

And they put it on the face of the old woman
Eee Nae Weyth
And there she could see what it was
It was an old man who had suffered
Eee Nae Weyth
He had suffered so much
Lt tee ooh na
Lt tee ooh na
Lt tee ooh na
Putting a dream over their soul.
Eee Nae Weyth
He was a lost soul
A doctoring man who took other people's pain out of their body
And he left them in his body
He tried to be stronger than his friends and relatives by taking
    on their pain
And by helping people this way he was asking the power to help
Eee Nae Weyth
He became so lost that the pain swallowed him up
Eee Nae Weyth
And she sang to the lost soul
She wore the clothes she put on it
And she said,
"Whoo wee whan shey la
"Hum shey la hum shey la."
Chant: Whoo wee whan han shey la, the soul will find itself by the
    doctoring person remembering that pain, calling that pain that they
    have felt in their life and how the patient is feeling, but is running
    from.
The doctoring person call the memory of that pain to feel it, to heal the
    patient.
Eee Nae Weyth
She hypnotized the spirit of pain
And she told the pain,

"He does not taste very good

"You want to throw him up

"He doesn't taste very good."

Eee Nae Weyth

And the spirit of pain was hypnotized by the old doctoring
woman and threw the man up

Eee Nae Weyth

There she poured water all over the clothes, herself

A bowl of water

And then she ran to the creek and bathed

Eee Nae Weyth

And it was like the clothes fell into a thousand pieces and floated
away

And as it floated she said,

"Eee lee wheeeee nee kai ooo

"Eee lee wheeeee nee kai ooo."

Eee lee wheeeee nee means the freeing of the soul.

Kai ooo means freeing of the universe or being one with the universe.

She said, "Your soul is free now

"Your soul is free

"It has gone back to the universe in thousands of pieces

"Thousands of pieces returning to the universe."

Eee Nae Weyth

And she could hear the Earth crying and crying for joy at the
comfort.

Eee Nae Weyth

And after that work she did

She said,

"Qwhee nah yah

"Qwhee yah nah

"Qulth thlae nae."

Qwhee nah yah means crying of happiness.

Qwhee yah nah is the crying of joy.

Qulth thlae nae is crying after everything is completed, like after

everything is done.
Eee Nae Weyth
She said, "Boy, that was hard work."
Boy that was hard work
And she wiped the sweat off her brow
Eee Nae Weyth
And there she told all the powers,
"I will have a feast."
Because the feast said, "I will have a feast."
Eee Nae Weyth
"I will have a feast because I have worked and travelled a long
    ways and I am hungry."
Eee Nae Weyth
And hungry agrees with me
And it says it wants a feast
And feast says it wants hunger
Eee Nae Weyth
And the spirit of want wants everything
And we have all agreed together to have a feast
Eee Nae Weyth
And a beautiful mat is made for these kinds of feasts
She tells her family and the weavers come together
And they weave a beautiful cloth
A cedar bark mat with beautiful designs of the journeys this old
    woman took
Eee Nae Weyth
And as they weave
They weave all the beautiful songs into this tablecloth
That is going to be used for the feast
Eee Nae Weyth
And she says to the people of the village,
"I only want hungry people to come."
Eee Nae Weyth
Thlee teee eene

Name of the hungry people spirit, spirit of all the hungry people.
And she says to the people of the village,
"I only want hungry people to come
"I only want people who love to eat to come."
Eee Nae Weyth
All the hungry people and all the people who love to eat agree
   with her
Eee Nae Weyth
And there as she is preparing the feast
She feels their appetites
And all their appetites are sitting around the tables before the
   people arrive
Eee Nae Weyth
And she knows where the people should be seated
Because she does not want to get their appetites mixed up with
   other people's
Eee Nae Weyth
And there they sang the table songs--the dinner songs
Ae nae naeth eee nehe naing nae
Name of dinner song.
People from all over the villages come
Because her village is all the people who are hungry and love to
   eat
Eee Nae Weyth
And when they sing the dinner songs it is the hunger that is
   singing
The hunger that is giving life force to emptiness
And the life force will be transformed into energy--food
Eee Nae Weyth
These dinner songs they sing
That is the spirit of hunger--of fasting
But it is also the spirit of fulfillment and good food
Eee Nae Weyth
Nee eulth seth thn

23

Translated in words that follow.
She has a beautiful feast
And beautiful songs
And she says, "Now we have eaten
"We have sang
"We need to hear the words of the people."
Eee Nae Weyth
And different words come out and are shared at the table
Eee Nae Weyth
And then they say to the words,
"We all agree with these words "
And we want these words to travel to the next generation."
Eee Nae Weyth
And these words agree they will travel to the next generation
Eee Nae Weyth
And the old people, they say,
"Nae halen na
"Nae halen nu san soo na
"Que whyoo en sun
"Ho hiyo sen sen."
Song translated in words that follow.
They are saying,
"We know why our clothes are wrinkled
"For we have worn them for a long time."
Eee Nae Weyth
Te ha neh nah eng eng kuse
Name of song.
And our clothes agree with us that they know why they are
 wrinkled for they have lived with us for a long time.
And then the doctoring woman she says as she gets up,
"Eth tee nee hae wee."
Summarized words of her powers.
As her hands are talking
That she is to point only up to the spirit of the universe

That the power of the universe is pointing at her
And she says,
"All my animal brothers and sisters, and aunties, and uncles
They are like my cane as I get older."
Eee Nae Weyth
"All the ones helped me travel
"All the ones showed me where to go
"The ones who are the birds the thunderbirds, the robin, the
    hummingbirds
"They show me how to fly in the right way
"Certain kinds of winds, certain kinds of storms only know how
    to fly in those storms
"And when I am traveling in the water
"Certain kinds of fish, certain kinds of whales seals, show me
    how to travel."
Eee Nae Weyth
"I have none of these powers because these powers are one
"We breathe the same air, we drink the same water, we use the
    same fire to heal one another."
And these are the words she gives to her powers
That she sings to her powers
Eee Nae Weyth
And she says, "I know what it is like to suffer
"I know what it is like to be healthy
"I know what it is like to feel pain
"I know what it is like to feel loneliness when there are lots of
    people around me
"Because I am the patient
"I am the healer
"We are one."
Eee Nae Weyth
And the people of the village would say about her, talk about
    her
Eee lem a when say ae

Aae lay thiey
Quen say ae lay
Ay lay aetay hay ae
Eee lem a when say ae is the soul of good and bad gossip mixed together.
Aye kay thiey is gossip to destroy someone.
Quen say ae lay is good gossip to heal someone.
Ay lay aelay hay ae is gibberish gossip, like people who talk but don't
    know anything.
Eee Nae Weyth
They say, "We know she likes to talk about herself all the time
    because she has lots of feasts all the time."
Eee Nae Weyth
"We know she talks about herself all the time
"That's why she has so much food on that table all the time."
Eee Nae Weyth
"We know she waits until our mouths are full so she can open
    her mouth that is empty."
Eee Nae Weyth
Ae flee nee ee tehth
Ae flee nee means my mouth is fasting.
Ee tehth means but my soul isn't fasting.
For the spirit of fasting
The spirit of emptiness
Is the same as the spirit of the great food
The good food of the table
Eee Nae Weyth
Quee eh len laee
The white canoe tablecloth or the white canoe altar.
The canoe, the white canoe, was the tablecloth
And there at the table everybody sees the canoe
The white canoe is the tablecloth
Eee Nae Weyth
The white canoe is the vision
The white canoe is the teacher

Eee Nae Weyth
The white canoe is the servant of the people
Eee Nae Weyth
Nee eee nail wealth
Eee ah nasil
Aa ya quan na sten
Sten nelth nea
Tune ya
Nee eee nail wealth are words for feelings of grandmothers of all canoes.
Aa is agreement, like yes.
Ya quan na sten is like shadows of my soul.
Sten nelth means the soul is pierced with the shadow.
Nea means traveling to.
Tune ya means my pain travels to the shadow, or darkness; could be good or bad. Traveling toward means good usually, but you never know.
Eee Nae Weyth
She tells the people about her next journey
How she will travel in her white canoe through the caves of the Earth
Eee Nae Weyth
Nee kam ah nay wah nae thlee
To be continued tomorrow.
The second night is the traveling through the Earth, the caves, the tunnels
The first night the doctoring woman has traveled through the waters as you have guessed
But all this time she has literally been traveling at the table
All the people who were sick, the suffering, the singers; the people who she had seen
Were around the table
That is what this white canoe is
They were all sitting at the table
So tomorrow night she will travel through the Earth

27

And these stories are so beautiful, the way they were sung by the old timers. I always admired the vitality and how much energy. These old people they would never seem to get tired of telling these stories. They would tell every little detail and they would repeat it five or seven times, that's why it took even longer, you know. That's why I am so glad I can translate it into English, shorten it and everything. But I tried to keep it traditional, I kept the sounds the same, singing the words. I never changed it, I kept it the same, I just didn't repeat the words five or seven times, that would be too long. And some of the words, the chanting, I didn't sing those because you have to go the full ten nights if you do that. I will shorten this story to three nights, maybe four, I am not sure, just because of time. I just thank each and every one for praying for these stories. Pray for the spirits and the ancestors that have been called in the stories to help us through the week. I thank each one for listening.

SECOND NIGHT

Yesterday, this medicine woman a very beautiful old woman who wears the clothes--the spirits--the souls as she travels. She traveled through the water. In this second part of the story as she travels to the first cave and she leaves her white canoe behind.

If you are listening to this story you can say Eee Nae Weyth
Eee Nae Weyth
Nee na tu iss eee
Wheee na ii nee
Ti kwe ti ke kew yeh
Ti kew nesten ieh
First line means the thoughts of the souls.
Second line means the thoughts of traveling in the souls.
Third line means souls' thoughts are the energy.
Fourth line means the souls' thoughts are the pathway.
Eee Nae Weyth
This old woman who is very beautiful
She tells the white canoe,
"I will let you rest now my dear one
"You have helped me so much
"It is time for me to enter the first cave."
Eee Nae Weyth
She enters the first cave
That is the west cave of the mountain
Eee Nae Weyth
She travels through this cave through a long tunnel
And her light is her hands
And her light is her eyes
Eee Nae Weyth
Whey naylem skwanee
Thee twae tem ka na

Whoon het kanan

First line means the thoughts that travel through the tips of the fingers.

Second line means the eyes traveling through the palm of your hand.

Third line like when you lay your hands on someone, your eyes see that part of the body.

Eee Nae Weyth

And the light tells her there has been someone that has been living in this rock called

Whill lee nee, whee lee nee kan say ah

Whill lee nee is the name of the rock.

Kan say ah means the rock is singing.

Eee Nae Weyth

This spirit has been living in this white rock that lives in the darkness

Eee Nae Weyth

And she sings a song, a power song, a doctoring song

Whee nee

Ee nee can

Thlee nae wee tee ten then

The first two lines mean the name of the power helpers of her doctoring song.

The third line means may the power show me the feelings of the souls.

Eee Nae Weyth

And the power says to her,

"This spirit, this white spirit will come out and it will be the clothes you will wear as you continue traveling through the tunnel."

Eee Nae Weyth

And she puts the clothes on

It is the soul of this spirit

And she puts it on and she feels these feelings

A feeling of great happiness

A great happiness that no one has ever seen

A person who had lived joy and had so much joy
But had never shared the joy with the people
Eee Nae Weyth
She wears this as she travels through the tunnel
She hears many songs in the tunnel
For there are many people who traveled through the tunnel for
    many generations
Eee Nae Weyth
She continues to sing her doctoring song
So that she is not distracted by the other songs
She continues to sing her doctoring songs
So the doctoring songs are not distracted by the other songs
Eee Nae Weyth
She continues singing so the singing will not be distracted by the
    other songs
Eee Nae Weyth
"Whee hai snae wee tee nee."

*Whee hai snae wee tee nee is a distracting doctoring song that distracts
other songs.*

*Te nee is the actual name of her doctoring song. The soul of the song
goes to the person while the distracting song is distracting other
songs. The belief is that even good songs can be distracting.*

And as she sings traveling through there
There is a cry that she hears in this tunnel
The upper part of the tunnel
And she feels in on the top of her head which is the entrance of
    the soul
Eee Nae Weyth
And her mind says,
"Wheee naeel si li
"Whan I can hun flesh
"Tee whesth ta lee."

Wheee naeel si li, her mind is connected with her soul.

Whan I can hun flesh, means I see what is going to come before me, I feel what is going to come.

Tee whesth ta lee means I choose this pathway to travel through.

Eee Nae Weyth

Her mind says, "Open the doorway

"Open the doorway to let this soul of this white spirit that you
  are wearing

"Let it out

"And return back to the crying spirit."

Eee Nae Weyth

So she opens the door and the door is this altar that she is
  wearing on her head

It is the white mountain goat cloth on top of her head

She takes that off and as she takes that off this soul travels out of
  the top of her head back to the spirit

Eee Nae Weyth

And the spirit begins to cry

Turns into laughter and the cry says,

"Fleeena hain swelt cun tal en nao wat tuen en nao."

Fleena is the cry of the underworld.

Hain swelt is the cry of the upper world.

*Tai en is the cry of the middle world. Like before you leave the Earth,
  like the aura of the Earth.*

Nao wat is the cry of the human heart.

*Tuen en nao is the cry of all lost souls that are stuck here on Earth,
  Demons too. Demons are just sick people.*

Eee Nae Weyth

The spirit says, "I have not been crying

"I have been laughing

"But the people on the outside of me only hear the crying

"They think I am crying, but I am laughing."

Eee Nae Weyth

The spirit is very happy

It has been healed

Been touched-

A demon

sitquen hut

A lying demon.

A demon whose work it was to kill people slowly to smother them with the cry

Eee Nae Weyth

And she asked the spirit

This demon, "Who are you?"

And it said, "I was one that once smothered people and now I am free.

"This was my punishment for smothering people for many generations

"And I spent many generations in this tunnel."

Eee Nae Weyth

As soon as the spirit said that

She could hear crying and laughter at the same time because the spirit was free and did not have to talk any more

Eee Nae Weyth

And she said,

"Whaaen aie ee

"Whaaen aie eee

"Teets ae whan ah."

Whaaen aie means my cry is healing my intent; my work.

Teets ae whan ah means the healing cry has agreed to live in my body.

Eee Nae Weyth

And she said, "That wasn't hard at all

"I didn't have to do anything

"It's so nice to work this way."

Eee Nae Weyth

And her doctoring song began to talk to her

And her power began to talk to her

Eee Nae Weyth

And the talk of the power began to talk to the power

And as it was talking and agreeing with one another it began again to talk to the old doctoring woman

Eee Nae Weyth

And the old doctoring woman, the old part of her body, began
to talk to the power

Eee Nae Weyth

And her soul began to talk to the power

And they began to agree on everything

Eee Nae Weyth

Eee nae tlth

Means they all agreed.

They all agreed

They all agreed

They said we must agree before the rest of her soul comes back
into her body

Eee Nae Weyth

This old woman's soul came back into her body and she says,

"See wheith can hai nee."

Means the soul is showing her where she has been.

"Where have I been?"

Eee Nae Weyth

And she told herself where she was

"I know where I have been."

Eee Nae Weyth

There she continues travelling into the tunnel

A whole person

Her soul was all together

Eee Nae Weyth

And her power said,

"There is another doctoring woman that is shooting a power
through the tunnel

"From the west door, the west entrance, the west gate."

Eee Nae Weyth

You must capture her poison that she is shooting

And she said to her power,

"If I capture this poison
"And I poison the poison then I will be in trouble."
Eee Nae Weyth
And there the power told her,
"Neeeish ta nee wa lae ne weyth
"Tae cann na ta naa sta tunae
"Whee wheelen noe whey whanna ta nae eee."
Whey whanna ta nae eee means the west cave is sending it mind, it's
power to the other powers to let them know what this woman is
doing.
And the power said,
"There is another doctoring woman that is shooting a power
through the tunnel from the west door, the west entrance, the
west cave."
Eee Nae Weyth
"You must let your power become the entrance
"For she is shooting her power
"She is going to try to change someone
"She is going to try to kill someone."
Eee Nae Weyth
"You must capture her poison that she is shooting."
And she said to her power,
"Whee nee whee leese ee nek quen nao whoon haey whoon
waey." *Translated in the following lines.*
And she said to the power,
"But if I capture this poison
"And I poison the poison
"Then I will be in trouble."
Eee Nae Weyth
And the power says,
"Eee nee quo len nae quo len neee eee."
Translated in the lines that follow.
It says,
"We will let the poison live in your bad thoughts

"And then your bad thoughts will die "And you will be safe."

Eee Nae Weyth

But she said again,

"But my bad thoughts live in my head

"And I do not want poison to leak out in my head."

She spent quite a bit of time arguing with the power

Back and forth

And the power said, "We have very little time left to argue

"You must agree with me now or be poisoned."

Eee Nae Weyth

And the story says.

"Whesh Hun."

Whesh Hun means just a second before the poison arrives she made herself a slave to the spirit.

Eee Nae Weyth

In other words, she decided at the last minute

Taneee tee heen eee haelae whee wha na ta non a staust when eee lae eee

Names of poison that comes from slave people, people that use their mind to degrade themselves.

Haelae whee is the name of slaves who choose not to see another way to live.

Wha na ta is a slave that chooses to be ruled by people.

Non a staust is a slave that chooses to be ruled by sick people that are demons.

When ee lee is the name of her slave power which is herself; her own bad thoughts; she chooses to be a slave to her own thoughts.

Eee Nae Weyth

And she could feel the poison enter through her left ear

And it entered her body

And she could feel great pain through her body

Eee Nae Weyth

And the poison said as it entered her body,

"Nae hon nae haun nae whey nae flae lae

"Nae hon hae haun lae flae swae nek cum say hae nae."
Translated in the lines that follow.
The power said,
 "I will really enjoy living in her
 "Will really enjoy drinking the blood of this doctoring woman
 "I will really enjoy sucking up all the breath she has in her body."
Eee Nae Weyth
And she wore the clothes of the poison
And she said, "These are nice clothes."
As she turned it inside out
And she sang her power song
And as she sang it began to rain in the tunnel
A great rain came down
This rain was very cold
Almost like hail, but not as cold, not as hard
Eee Nae Weyth
And she said,
"Nee lee wee han nae won say won
"Say nae wee sen tan ten
"Saeel hun set eel a hun nat."
Nee lee wee han nae won say won means who is crying (the rain.)
The rain says it is the birds, the spiritual bird.
Say nae wee sen tan ten means all the white birds that are crying,
    singing.
Saeel hun set eel a hun nat means the tunnel belongs to these birds.
It is the mind. The universe of these birds that are different kinds of
    people.
The birds are people. They were teaching her through the singing.
Eee Nae Weyth
And as she sang she could hear thousands of birds
Little white birds, white hummingbirds
Flying through the tunnel
They were coming towards her
Eee Nae Weyth

And they flew right through her
These were souls of people who died on the Earth
Eee Nae Weyth
These were souls that were stuck in the Earth
That were free because this doctoring woman captured this
  poison
Eee Nae Weyth
There she had saved one person
By capturing this poison
But thousands of people died
Thousands of people were freed
People who were ready to die
But they were captured by their relatives and friends.
Eee Nae Weyth
And she said to these clothes of poison,
"I am finished now
"I am done with you."
Eee Nae Weyth
And there she heard a little boy singing
As she continued walking into the tunnel
And the little boy that was singing must have been nine years
  old.
And the boy said,
"Hay nae aun
"Hae noe hanee whee aun
"Haun nee whee aun noe aun."
Translated in the words that follow.
Eee Nae Weyth
The little boy was saying,
"I am a power;
"I am a power waiting for a master
"Waiting for my master to give me one more order
"One more order to heal someone."
Eee Nae Weyth

"And then I will be free."
And there she sang over the poison she was still wearing on her
    body
And she said,
"Return to the power
"Return to the spirit you belong to."
Eee Nae Weyth
And the little boy disappeared
For that was the power that belonged to the little boy
Ne thee thils
Name of boy.
Another soul that was freed again
And she continued and she said to herself,
"Ae kan nee nea ea ea."
Translated in the lines that follow.
She said, "I am tired of traveling through this tunnel."
Eee Nae Weyth
When she said that all through the tunnel it sighed and moaned
Eee Nae Weyth
It was a moaning sound
She followed this moaning sound
And the moaning sound said,
"Hoooo yah ooooh wha nat."
Translated in lines that follow.
It said, "Ooh I will help you get out of here."
Eee Nae Weyth
It was a moaning sound and she followed this moaning sound
And the moaning sound belonged to a doctoring woman who
    lived in the east side of the mountain
Who was a moaning doctor
Eee Nae Weyth
She followed the moaning sound and there was the moaning
    doctor and she said,
"Oh wee thee nee tee na

"Hana ka nee hee nee hee eee eee."
Translated in the following lines.
Eee Nae Weyth
She said, "Ooo thank you for getting me out of the west tunnel
"That west cave.
"You are the moaning doctor."
And the moaning doctor said—moaning,
"Ahhaa haa la qua."
"I am, yeah."
Eee Nae Weyth
And the moaning doctor said,
"Everyone thinks the east is a bright and wonderful place,
"A place of growth
"And a place where the sun rises,
"But not in the mountain."
Eee Nae Weyth
"For the sun tells the people to be refreshed
"To be renewed
"But the sun leaves us all the left-over work."
Moan
Eee Nae Weyth
"I am the guardian of the east side of the mountain
"I am the moaning doctor
"I will moan your sickness to death."
Eee Nae Weyth
"Eenah nah wah na way na nah hae."
Translated in lines that follow.
(Moaning) "I am the moaning doctor.
"I will moan you to death.
"I am the one who will moan you to death.
"I am the moaning doctor
"I will moan for your pains."
Eee Nae Weyth
(Moaning) "I am the moaning doctor

"I will moan for all your complaints."

Eee Nae Weyth

(Moaning) "I am the moaning doctor

"I will moan for all the people you hate."

Eee Nae Weyth

(Moaning) "And I will enjoy every moaning minute."

Eee Nae Weyth

She sang her doctoring song that sounded really different

"Haaa ouooouu awaaaa nee ha whaaa nae wha naee

"Wha hae ka nae ka naw."

Means my moaning is the moaning of all my ancestor spirits that I
  don't like. That is why I am moaning.

Eee Nae Weyth

And the beautiful old doctoring woman said,

"The moaning makes you feel like it is many generations old."

Eee Nae Weyth

The moaning doctoring woman said, (moan)

"Ahhhha ou."

Translated in the next line.

Eee Nae Weyth

The moaning doctor says, "It is very old."

Eee Nae Weyth

Thee na heet na na hah

Wheut ka nah swet

Translated in the following line.

The moaning doctoring woman, she says,

"I get my relief by traveling with the wind."

Eee Nae Weyth

She travels to the north, to the south, the west, and the east
  through the wind

And her voice is very beautiful in the wind

But it is a very painful moan

Et Ken

Name of painful moan.

Eee Nae Weyth

And the old doctoring woman, she says,

"The power says to me to give you this song to help you."

Eee Nae Weyth

The moaning doctor says (moan,)

Eee Nae Weyth

The moaning doctoring woman says (moaning,)

"Ooh hay naa hoou han ou ee oo."

"Thank you. Thank you very much. Oh thank you very, very, very much."

Eee Nae Weyth

The moaning doctor says, "Ooohhh thank you."

Eee Nae Weyth

And sings the song and washes away the heaviness of the moaning doctor

And the moaning doctoring woman is free

Eee Nae Weyth

Leaving her power to the next one who is going to be lucky to guard the east side of the mountain

Eee Nae Weyth

And the doctoring woman says,

"So that's why they say not to travel to the other side of the mountain

And why they say to be careful on a vision quest not to go too far or you might be the guarding of the eastern mountain."

Eee Nae Weyth

And she realized that she was the only one at the eastern side of the mountain.

That the moaning doctor woman tricked her

Eee Nae Weyth

But her other power that she had was called

Quea Laan eee

Translated in following line.

Eee Nae Weyth

Her other power was called
Too stupid to know
Eee Nae Weyth
And she called the powers of stupidity
The powers of nothingness
And she says,
"Que ahn nook poos kaus."
*Poos kaus means the dumb spirits. They live everywhere because they
do not know where the dumb world is. There is a dumb world but
the dumb spirits don't even know where it is.*
"I am so stupid and dumb
"We do not want disaster to happen to the Earth because of our
stupidity."
Eee Nae Weyth
And there a great wind pushes her out of the east tunnel into the
south part of the mountain
Eee Nae Weyth
And the south part of the mountain is a really beautiful place
It is like being in the universe
It is very, very bright
The bright part of the universe
Eee Nae Weyth
There it is summer all the time
There are no seasons there
Eee Nae Weyth
There her power sings and it says,
"En doan ah felalen doana telan nae ee nee
"Toe quats aye ya nat ah tha then quae sa elth
"Fleeth tan quan tum sa ee."
Translated in the following lines.
Eee Nae Weyth
The power says,
"We have brought you here to the south cave
"To help us because we are having too much fun here

"We are having too much brightness
"We cannot stand it any longer."
Eee Nae Weyth
They were misplaced spirits
They were forced to go the happy, sunny place of the mountain
Misplaced spirits that were trying to be miserable on Earth
Trying to do their job
They were just trying to a good job of being miserable
And were forced to go to this nice place
Eee Nae Weyth
And the miserable spirit said (song sung miserably,)
"Eee nee eee wee ee neu
"Hk hk nee neeha nee hk."
Translated in the following line. Eee Nae Weyth
(Said in miserable tone) "OOOH could you please help us find
    our miserable way?"
Eee Nae Weyth
The beautiful old doctoring woman couldn't believe it
These people, so handsome, so beautiful
But they were miserable spirits
Eee Nae Weyth
And she received the clothes
Their souls and she put them on and she said to them,
"Eee ne eeena ee qua na ee."
*Eee ne eeena ee means it wants you. It wants you. Like a spiritual
    knowledge; wanting to receive spiritual knowledge.*
*Qua na ee means she is putting this knowledge into them so they can
    understand.*
"There is a miserable human being who is wanting you
"There is a miserable human being 100 miles away on a vision
    quest who needs you right now."
Eee Nae Weyth
So in other words, she was sicking these miserable spirits on
    human beings who were going on vision quests

Eee Nae Weyth

And the miserable spirits would shoot through their body and
they would be miserable for a minute or so

And that's how those spirits were freed from the Earth.

Eee Nae Weyth

And she thought she was done

But there in the corner of this cave

In the very corner

In the tiniest crack of the cave

Eee Nae Weyth

There was a little mouse

And the little mouse was the underworld mouse

And she said (mouse voice,)

"Nee wee ween ahh quee neeng nne naung quee."

Translated in the following lines.

"Oh, please can you help this miserable spirit to find a human
being?

"It's keeping us up all night."

Eee Nae Weyth

And so the old doctoring woman she helped the underworld
mouse

And they sang together

And there they sent that spirit to another person

Who was on a vision quest on this mountain

Eee Nae Weyth

And her work was done in the southern cave

Eee Nae Weyth

She started walking through this tunnel

And as she walked through the tunnel

She heard a beautiful song

This man that was singing to her

Eee Nae Weyth

"Hay nah eee yahh whey lay um ahhn."

Hay nah eee yahh whey is translated in the following lines.

Lay um ahhn is the name of this spirit.
Eee Nae Weyth
And the voice said, "I am the one that controls all the creeks and
    the rivers and the waterfalls on the mountain."
Eee Nae Weyth
"I am the one who decides how clean a person needs to be."
Eee Nae Weyth
"I am the one who decides how thirsty they need to be."
Eee Nae Weyth
"And I am the one who decides whether they should drown or
    not."
Eee Nae Weyth
And within the voice were many souls that were captured
That were drowned in the creeks, in the rivers
Eee Nae Weyth
And she asked this voice,
"Why do you keep the souls in your voice?"
And the voice spoke to her just with sound
And she realized what he was
A power of the universe
And she said,
"Te eel lee nee whan na
"Ta kash klee kalan ta tan at
"Ta ats a han an nat."
Translated in the lines that follow.
That the voice captures the souls of people
Drowns them in the creeks
Drowns them in the rivers
When we decide they are not going to do their work
Eee Nae Weyth
And she laughed and laughed
She thought that was funny
For she was a doctoring woman
Na hah na ha ta nat ten

Na hah na means the laughter from above, the sky world.
Ha ta means the laughter from all directions, a circle around me.
And her laughter laughed and laughed
Because it knew she was a doctoring woman
Eee Nae Weyth
And the doctoring laughed
Because it knew she was a doctoring woman
Eee Nae Weyth
And of course, the old woman laughed and laughed
Because she knew she was a doctoring woman
Eee Nae Weyth
They all agreed that she was a doctoring woman
And they all laughed together
Eee Nae Weyth
And as she sings the song
It is all the creeks, rivers, waterfall
The tears of all the people were laughing together
As they were seeing themselves
As they heard the old woman's song
They saw themselves as they were
Ever in that moment of drowning
Eee Nae Weyth
And they all laughed together
And the voice did not think it was funny that she was laughing
And he became angry.
And as it became angry the souls escaped from his voice
And they appeared in the creeks and the rivers and the waterfalls
To the human beings and the animals and the plants that were
    there
Eee Nae Weyth
And each of those elements
Each of those life forces, life breaths
Captured the souls that appeared
And saved them and freed them

And returned them back to the human beings

Eee Nae Weyth

There the voice said now,

"Whe lan aaiee enna."

Means I do not want to start all over looking for souls.

The voice said, "Now I have to start all over."

"Ka nee wa thing."

Means now I have to start all over.

"Looking for more souls."

Eee Nae Weyth

And the spirit says, "This is the work of the elements to find lost souls."

If they discontinue working

Then it would be the end of the world

Eee Nae Weyth

"Lahee nee fee lee nee tee ka leee nee."

She is traveling, she is saying the tunnel is showing me the next direction to go.

And as she traveled through the tunnel

Eee Nae Weyth

And now it will change and you will say Eeeee Naaee Weyth

Eeeee Naaee Weyth

Now there as she traveled through this tunnel

She heard many voices of children singing and laughing and talking

Eeeee Naaee Weyth

And she listened to these voices

And as she listened to them, she asked these voices,

"Why am I hearing you?"

And her hearing said,

"Why am I hearing you?"

And her hearing and self agreed

That they were hearing the voices

And the voices said,

"Why are you listening to us?"
And they all agreed they could hear each other
Eeeee Naaee Weyth
The na nee te the lee tiss
The souls of the universe hear us and our souls hear the universe.
They were voices of souls
That were coming to the Earth,
But had not reached the Earth yet
Now this is where you could hear the voices of the souls
Who are coming in the north cave of this mountain
Eeeee Naaee Weyth
She found the entrance
And was sucked to the bottom of the mountain
And she went to the underworld cave of the mountain
Eeeee Naaee Weyth
This is where you say
Eee Naaae Thleep (Slow and deep)
We are listening in the underworld
Eee Naaae Thleep
There she traveled in the underworld cave. It was very bright
    down there
Very beautiful
Eee Naaae Thleep
Eee nee willa banee wee teeea
Translated in the following lines.
Where all the animals talk like human beings
And all the human beings talk like the animals
Eee Naaae Thleep
And she met this bear that lived
The underworld bear
The bear said,
"Laah wael la qua la."
"I am hungry."
Eee Naaae Thleep

The bear said,
"I am hungry."
Eee Naaae Thleep
She laughed and laughed at the bear
And he held out his paw
And food of all kinds started falling out of his hands
And she looked at his paws and she screamed
And as she screamed the bear fell over and died
Eee Naaae Thleep
It was the leader of the Underworld Bear People
And this is how he was supposed to die.
He was waiting for this old doctoring woman
Eee Naaae Thleep
And there she knew her work was done
Eee Naaae Thleep
And she continued
And she seen another animal there
And this animal was a human being
Eee Naaae Thleep
But the human being
It spoke like a bear
Eee Naaae Thleep
And she screamed at this human being
And this human being went to sleep
Eee Naaae Thleep
And he started to dream and dream
And she could see the dream and the dream said,
"Nael kunama tuah na han."
Translated in the following lines.
Eee Naaae Thleep
"Nael kalum ka ha na."
Translated in the following lines.
It said, "The paws, the bear's paws, grab them
"Cut the paws off the bear."

Eee Naaae Thleep
And she said, "What will I cut them off with?"
And there they said, "With your hands."
And there she looked at her hands and they were like knives
And there she cut the paws off
Eee Naaae Thleep
And the dream said, "Sing over them now
"And it will be received by someone on this mountain
"Someone that is on this mountain who is sleeping now."
Eee Naaae Thleep
And there she sang over them
And she saw this power travel to this person who was sleeping
    on this mountain.
Who was going to be a doctoring woman
Eee Naaae Thleep
She would be an herbal doctor
And she would have the paws to dig any kind of roots because
    the bears have paws to dig
Eee Naaae Thleep
And the bears loved flowers and the plants
Little tiny flowers
Little tiny flowers would dance around and laugh at them
Eee Naaae Thleep
And there she received this gift
Na han na teet ta la la tutish
Na han na teet is the name of tiny flowers.
Ta la la tutish means every kind of plant, herbal plants.
Now you can go back to Eee Nae Weyth
Eee Nae Weyth
And there she knew that she would be sucked up to the upper
    world of the mountain
The very, very top
Where none of the human beings go
The white mountain top

Eee Nae Weyth
And there this place
It's a place for only the very old doctoring people
Eee Nae Weyth
And in this place
She hears songs
That she had never heard before.
From another time
Another place
Eee Nae Weyth
And the snow and ice they sing to her
And they sing beautiful songs
And they tell her of things that have happened
How the people came
They sing the songs of memory
They sing the songs of thoughts and feelings
That were left in the ice by the ancestors
Eee Nae Weyth
And these are feelings and thoughts
That are gathered in the vision quests by the people
Eee Nae Weyth
And then the old doctoring woman
She looks down the mountain
And she knows she is inside the mountain,
But she can see outside
And she looks down and she sees
Oh, so it is
That the mountains are like the minds of the Earth
The mountains are like the brain of the Earth
Eee Nae Weyth
There she follows this feeling
Leaving the top of the mountain going down
Haa ahh haa ah
The sound of the mountain's mind

It is like a humming sound
A continuous humming sound she hears
Following it down the mountain
And she knows it is the song of this mountain
The side of the mountain
Eee Nae Weyth
And she says,
"No one sees the sides of the mountain
"Only the blind people do."
Eee Nae Weyth
And as she travels down them
She becomes very happy
As she knows her work is almost done
Traveling in these tunnels and caves
Eee Nae Weyth
But there again she gets very sleepy half way down the mountain
And she's pulled right into the center of the mountain
Eee Nae Weyth
The center of the cave
And this is where a power of ego
The power of thoughts and strength live
Eee Nae Weyth
She in the center
In the great part of the mountain
In the cave there is an old man
And the old man says,
"Aye na na han nae haas."
Translated in the following lines.
Eee Nae Weyth
"I am the center of all
"I am the center of all ego."
Eee Nae Weyth
"I am the biggest ego you have ever seen."
Eee Nae Weyth

And this old doctoring woman starts giggling and giggling.
She just can't stop giggling
She thinks it's so silly
Eee Nae Weyth
She says to herself,
She sings to herself,
"Nee hee hee hee quan hee
"Nee hee hee
"Nee Quan hee."
Second line means her giggling, her giggling power.
Third line means hoping his head, his ego will explode.
"Not only the biggest ego I have ever seen
"But the biggest head I have ever seen."
Eee Nae Weyth
And there she notices he is wearing a really beautiful ring
On the top of his head
A cedar bark ring
It is shiny, very, very shiny
Light coming out of this ring
Like a little halo maybe
And she asks him,
"What is that little ring you are wearing on top of your head?"
And he says,
"Whey la na hay."
Translated in the next line.
"That is not my ring it is my head band."
Eee Nae Weyth
His head is so big
But the headband is so tiny
And she laughs again
And laughs and laughs and laughs
And he begins to fade away
Eee Nae Weyth
He disappears (explodes)

And she looks around
And the power says
Her power,
"He has not disappeared. He is here."
Eee Nae Weyth
Power of ego says,
"I have not disappeared
"I am so huge you cannot see me."
Eee Nae Weyth
And she begins to laugh again
Laughing and laughing
The ego cannot stand this old doctoring woman
And says,
"Lay na mao nee na whee na mao."
Translated in the following lines.
Eee Nae Weyth
"I must not allow my ego to get any smaller
"So you must leave."
Eee Nae Weyth
And she wonders what the purpose of this cave is
The center cave of the mountain
Eee Nae Weyth
And this power that is used, it says,
"Whel kan nees whan ah nah whal ah nal la han san tan."
Translated in the following lines.
"We are used in the songs
"We are used in the doctoring songs
"We are used to protect the ones who are working."
Eee Nae Weyth
The egos are used like fences are used
Eee Nae Weyth
To keep destructive forces out
This is how the power of ego is used
Eee Nae Weyth

And the old doctoring woman thought to herself,
"Quee nee na nah eele."
Translated in the following line.
"Not anymore." (Small voice.)
Eee Nae Weyth
People have learned to become weak
Because of ego
They do not know how to use egos
As healing power
Eee Nae Weyth
There she begins to travel away from the center of the mountain
Eee Nae Weyth
Th aye nay hay la hat ta ten whee nae lay ha nae suken
Translated in the following lines.
And there she finds herself
Very, very tired
And she says to herself,
"I am so very tired."
Eee Nae Weyth
And her power says, "I am so tired."
Eee Nae Weyth
And her mind says, "I am so tired."
Eee Nae Weyth
And her tiredness says, "I am so tired."
Eee Nae Weyth
They are so tired they cannot even agree
But they know they are tired
Eee Nae Weyth
She falls asleep and awakens again
And she finally finds herself in the entrance
The west entrance of the mountain
Eee Nae Weyth
Thelee nee lee theee quae lee nee thee
Helee nee lee is the name of a crystal in a cave.

Theee quae lee is the name of blue, purplish and white crystal that lives
in a cave in the mountain.
Nee thee means beautiful clear crystals.
And this beautiful cave has all crystals in there
And she looks around Beautiful clear crystals
Eee Nae Weyth
And the crystals say,
"We are the Earth star people
"We are the ones who are helping the Earth."
Eee Nae Weyth
There she looks at them
She touches these crystals
And each one she touches
She receives knowledge from
Eee Nae Weyth
And then she realizes why doctoring people
Only carry rock people
Any kind of rocks
Crystals
Only to carry knowledge
To someone else
To give it away
Eee Nae Weyth
Never keep it for yourself
Because the knowledge will kill you
Eee Nae Weyth
And as she was leaving this cave she thought,
"Whoo nee teeee eo kalee nee."
Whoo nee teeee means the light of the crystal will transport your soul
to another dimension; time. The crystal will show you how to do
that.
Eo kalee nee is the name of that particular crystal that helps you travel
in this way.
Eee Nae Weyth

She thinks to herself,
"Boy that was such a long journey through that mountain."
Eee Nae Weyth
"I can't wait to get back to my white canoe."
And there she gets sleepy again
She falls asleep four times
The fifth time she awakens
Eee Nae Weyth
And this fifth time she awakens she notices people all around
    her
Eee Nae Weyth
Real big people
Heavy set people
Eee Nae Weyth
And she says to them,
"Why are you folks around me?"
These people were saying,
"We're singing for the mountain doctoring people."
Eee Nae Weyth
And she thought they weren't the mountain doctoring people
    because they were so heavyset
So huge and so big
Eee Nae Weyth
And they said,
"No "Those people over there
"Who have been doctoring over you
"They are the mountain doctoring people."
Eee Nae Weyth
And she looked at them
And they were the skinniest, scroungiest looking doctoring
    people she had ever seen
Eee Nae Weyth
Then she knew she must have been dreaming
She thought she was traveling through that mountain

Eee Nae Weyth
She closed her eyes and opened them again
And there she found herself on the west side of the mountain
Eee Nae Weyth
And she looked around
And she seen boulders
It was the singers I guess
And she looked around
And she saw some scroungy looking trees
Eee Nae Weyth
Those must have been the doctoring people
She did not ask any more questions
She continued walking
To get away from this mountain
Eee Nae Weyth
And she did not say she wished
That she would see her white canoe again
Because she was afraid she might black out again
Eee Nae Weyth
And she knew if she wished she could be at her home
She would have to work again
Eee Nae Weyth
Qua nee lee tee neee tee nee
Qua nee lee tee is the exhausting power song.
Neee tee nee means exhausted from singing this song.
Eee Nae Weyth
And she was so exhausted she said to herself,
Eee Nae Weyth
"I am so exhausted." (tiredly)
Eee Nae Weyth
"I am so exhausted." (more tiredly)
Eee Nae Weyth
"I am so exhausted." (yawning)
Eee Nae Weyth

"I am so exhausted." (more yawning)
Eee Nae Weyth
And she fell asleep
Th neee lee na hee Means exhausted
And she saw the mountain
And the mountain said,
"Wake up."
Eee Nae Weyth
And she awakened
And there she was
Sitting at the table at her white canoe
Eee Nae Weyth
And she looked around
And there were people who brought food
And some got up and they said,
"I got this deer from the west side of the mountain."
Eee Nae Weyth
And someone got up and said,
"I gathered these roots on the north side of the mountain."
Eee Nae Weyth
And someone said,
"I got this water from the creek
"And I felt my soul returning to me."
Eee Nae Weyth
And there she looked around
All the people were gathered around the white canoe
The white canoe is the table as well
The table we eat at
Eee Nae Weyth
And then someone got up and said,
"I am preparing to travel to the mountain."
Eee Nae Weyth
And the beautiful old doctoring woman got up and said,
"I've had enough."

Eee Nae Weyth
And again she blacked out
And found herself back at the west side of the mountain
Eee Nae Weyth
And they all said to her,
"Oh nat ten."
Translated in the following line.
"You're back again."
Eee Nae Weyth
As soon as she said, "Yes."
They said, "We have had enough."
Eee Nae Weyth
And she awakened again
She was back at the table with the people eating
Eee Nae Weyth
And she thought to herself,
"I can't wait until the feast is done."
Eee Nae Weyth
The nee tee kan ten
Translated in the following line.
The old doctoring woman continued travelling
And she said to herself,
"I must prepare to talk to my white canoe."
Eee Nae Weyth
She said to the white canoe,
"Where shall we travel next?"
Eee Nae Weyth
And it said,
"Quae quae quae lay nae."
Meaning the fire coming out of the thunderbird's mouth and eyes.
The thunderbird also has to do with lightening and fire.
Eee Nae Weyth
"We will travel to the fire
"To the many fires of the Earth, and spirit, and air spirit."

Eee Nae Weyth

Te ka ha na tet au toot sweet ka nae to haut ka

Naut ten len ta ten ta nae wae stelth ta ha ha nan et

Ta now wa steelth ta ka a snaee te ta ta howet stelth

Te wilth ne

Te ka ha na tet means Earth. Au toot sweet ka means spirit.

To haut ka naut ten means air. Traveling out to the many fires of the Earth.

To the many fires of the spirit. Traveling out to the many fires of the air... Nae wae stelth ta means talking about the songs/experiences in the several hours of the story that were skipped. Experiences of the fire traveling out.

Ha ha nan is the name of the song and of the air traveling out.

Et ta now wa means in the story it talks of the doctoring songs of the elements.

Steelth ta ka a is the name of the song repeated.

Steth tee wilth ne is the name of the spirit of the fire, the story about that.

And there are several hours of this story that I did not tell. And a lot of songs that are not sung, doctoring songs. Now she is going to travel to the fire now--land of fire--spirit of fire.

That's the third part of the story where she will travel. In this story she has travelled through the mountains.

The old people tell us the mountain is a place and time. It is a universe that is within your own soul that we call the mountain. The mountain you are drawn to, the space and time we are drawn to, that physical mountain is that space living in your own soul. It is the same space, the same time that your ancestors, someone who had sought a way of healing other people, they went to that same place.

In the story, this old doctoring woman, she travels to many places that her own ancestors traveled to. And so, in the story, in the native language, they have different names for different thoughts. This is where she has travelled to. Different thoughts that she was going through in her own mind and soul before she reaches her destination in the cave. The person she is going to pray for, the person she is going to heal or free. She goes through different thoughts. In the story was pain, different feelings were felt, frustration, being tired, these were thoughts, her own thoughts that lived within her soul. So, she was travelling to herself in the story.

In the native language they have words for those things. In this story, the second part of the story, the old people say now we have traveled forward and backward the second part is backward. Now we will travel to the right and to the left. The third part will be to the right and the fourth part will be the left part of the soul.

And the doorways, the four doorways doctoring people talk about, are the doorway to the front, the back, the sides. And these are songs. Songs from those directions. Doorways, the people, say are songs from those directions.

If you listen to the story in the way it was sung, certain tones, certain ways, that is the direction. In the olden days when they would sing these stories the epic storyteller would even face the direction of the story they were telling. That kind of went out the window during my mother's time. She said it went out in the fifties. Oh, so much for the stories, let's just tell the stories. And as time goes on, we are getting more and more modern and people are not having time to tell these stories. Like today they have done away with a lot of the ritual of the way they would tell the story, this particular story of the woman, the beautiful old doctoring woman who wears the clothes, the many souls, and many elements.

In this story Grandmother told me, a storyteller, a really good story teller who studied the epic stories, would tell it in the old language, epic story telling language. And they would tell it four or five times and the last part of the story, the last hour of the story, was repeated seven times. I heard this when I was a child. As I was older a lot of the old timers would talk about it and say that is how some of the old timers would tell it and we are kind of lazy. If they were lazy, we are really lazy now. I just wanted to share that with you so you could get the feeling of what it must have been like to have to stay there, camp for a week or so, ten nights, four nights, whatever it was.

The last time I heard the story my uncle Alex, from Esquimalt, Songhees, told the story in 1977. He had three singers, story tellers, epic story tellers who always had trained singers to help them tell the stories. So, as he was telling the story, the singers would sing different parts of the voices, it was so beautiful to hear that. As I got older, as a teenager, a lot of the older people were dying and none of the young people kept it up so we have lost it. It is sad that it is gone now.

I remember that the best epic singers were from Kayuga, Ah Hat Ta Thia, *Cedar Bark Societies*. And there were epic singers from Kwakwala people from Cape Cook. They were neighbors to the Checklasaht people and the Ohiat. And there was one epic story teller from Bamfield, B.C. that died in 1975. They called him Choppy. His last name was Tatoosh, he was Sdakalanee Tatoosh or Timothy Tatoosh or Tatoosh and he was a wonderful epic teller. He had four singers that would sing with him. He only told seven-night stories or ten-night stories.

He was one of my teachers as a child. My grandfather would make me go with him to Bamfield and he would say, "You're going to learn this story now." And every hour my grandfather would say, "You're going to learn this story now." It was like he was hypnotizing me or something. He would say that every hour. As they were telling the stories my grandfather would interrupt and say, "You are going to learn the story now."

As the story teller was telling the story I would keep on going and I would think in my mind, "I am learning the story now." And after a while he realized how my mind was and I kept on memorizing. "I am going to learn the story." For seven nights I heard that every hour. After a time, my grandfather stopped interrupting me and just would look at me so I didn't miss the one minute or two minutes of the story while he was interrupting. Those are the memories I have as I am telling the stories now.

I think of all those old people who are gone now. It is so sad that many of our people have lost that now and it is even worse here. Grandma Ivy was telling me in her time there were lots of tellers. They lost the epic tellers here a lot earlier compared to Canada. The story telling, when you tell the stories, the people believed they could get healed at a story telling.

People believed in those days. The tiredness, the purpose of getting tired at an epic story. People would say, "I am going to purposely get tired." They used to have to tell themselves, that's how strong they were. They had to say, "I know I am going to get tired." They were looking forward to getting tired at a story telling. The part of themselves that was sick or troubled would get tired and fall asleep and when they would wake up, they would leave it behind. That was their way of thinking, the old timers. My grandmother used to say "Oh, I just can't wait to go to that ten-night story telling I know a lot of sicknesses are going to fall asleep and be left behind there." It is just so funny how they used to think. That's all gone now. I just wanted to share that with you so when you are getting tired you can think of that your troubles are the ones that are getting tired and going to fall asleep and when you wake up you will leave them behind.

Let the stories take care of them

Nee ha ha lam tee hail weth neth

The name of the story,

Of the teachings,

Of why they are going through their experiences and getting tired and angry and happy.

And what all that means.

For the closing part of this the weavers were so wonderful. The weavers, the basket weavers were so magical, I always thought they were magical when I was a little, watching these old ladies and also elderly men. It always seemed to be old people that would be weaving. There was one of my aunts, she was my auntie and she was a couple years older than I was. She was the youngest person I ever saw weaving during the epic story telling. She would weave.

These kinds of weavers would weave all the designs of the story into the basket during that time. And then they would bury it. Bury it. Or then they would burn the basket at the ending of the epic story telling. That is something we have lost too. They don't do that anymore. Then if a design was given out from the basket the weaver would pick someone in the story, point at him, she'd sing her song having her finger pointed upward at him. She would go around and then she'd point at the person and say "you will give a potlatch for the one design and you tell the people why and you will tell the people the meaning of the design."

And the person had to really listen to the story because if they fell asleep in that part of the story, they would have to ask someone else "what was the design, what was the meaning of that, I wasn't awake for that one." They would have to give a potlatch because a weaver would tell them to at the last minute. One of those last-minute potlatches.

The whole family would get together scramble around and try to get things together and invite people to their house. And then after the potlatch then they would finish with what they would call the sister to that story, the twin sister. They had twin sister stories. It was only twin sisters and twin brother stories which are forty-night stories. Twenty nights they tell it then the design is given away and then the person finally has a potlatch and then they have twenty more nights. And people gather and feast before and after the stories. Those are fun, a lot of fun.

You know a lot of our native people who were assimilated into the white man's world. In the background sometimes you hear TV; Gilligan's Island. Someone, one of the kids, was watching TV. But there all the traditional people would fill the living room or fill the room, kitchen, wherever the epic storytelling was held, so many people. Even with all the noises in the background, telephone going off and everything, people were just concentrating on the storytelling. Such a wonderful experience to have that.

The only time the epic story telling was interrupted was if there was a death. If someone died, a relative or friend in the village, then everything would stop and they would pay witnesses. They would always pick witnesses and tell those witnesses after the funeral is over "we will finish our work with the epic story telling." And they would ask forgiveness of all those story tellers, ancestor story tellers who told these stories. "Forgive us we can't tell this, The Great Spirit called our loved one, they were the one who interrupted our story. They were always known to interrupt everything." And that's the way the old people talked, "Oh gosh that person got us at their last breath, bothering us all our life when they were alive. They did one more job, they interrupted one more ceremony with their death while we were enjoying ourselves." And that's the way they talked, those old people and it was so funny to hear them talk that way.

And these epic stories, many of them, mostly northern and middle Nootka, you never heard any English at all. It was all in the native language, or Salish or Hulkameelum. A lot of Cowichan people would travel over for these epics. A lot of them were epic tellers from Cowichan and a few from Saanich, not too many, and southern Nootka. When you get to Didanat, or Nitinat, Port Alberni, those southerners down there, they would always have some English in the epic storytelling, with pieces of English heard. And then if there was a lot of young people there, they would always have a translator.

Their epic story telling was much longer because they had to stop and translate all into English for the young people who did not speak the language. So it was even longer for those kinds of storytelling and the old people used to say that someday you will look back at this and say to yourself "I'm glad I was there" and as you say that words will go into the sacred breath and the breath will have pity on the people who want the ancient ceremonies to survive and they will be revived with the new breath. And the old people said that first you had to learn the songs and sing all the songs and then sing all the words.

It's just really wonderful we can bring these stories out up here at the medicine house, the mother house. Old lady Adde was a wonderful person. She told epic stories. She was the only epic teller that would cuss in the middle of her epic. If she was reminded of someone who owed her money or someone, she was mad at or someone who said something to her she'd start cussing right there in the middle of storytelling. After she got done relieving herself cussing, getting mad at the person, she'd return to the story telling. But she put everyone through her cussing. People would take breaks you know, that was the only epic teller that I knew that was like that. Aunt Philomena was a little bit different. She always waited 'til she was done with her work and in some ways that was worse. This much I have to share.

I want to thank each and every one for listening to this long story and just wanted to explain from here to there so we can get a better feeling of the story and pray for the story and pray for the work that this particular story is coming out now. I don't know why certain stories come out. Maybe we will never know. Maybe the next generation will know.

Johnny Moses brought out this story at Swinomish in 1994.

THIRD NIGHT

Last night in the story we were sharing of the beautiful old doctoring woman traveling to the mountain, traveling through the prayers through the Earth. Now in the third part of the story she travels to the light. There are many different levels of light and fire in the story. Fliat is the light, Holy light, Sacred light. The light, old people say that when we are born into this world it is the light that materializes, that it is the light of Grandmother Earth that gives us the body of Mother Earth. We are born to Grandmother Earth; it materializes this body it comes to us. It materializes and we are lights.

In the language they have many different ways for different kinds of light. There is dark light, grey light, different shades of light. Many of us are made of different kinds of light depending on where we have travelled and where we have travelled from, which direction we will have been, which kinds of lights surrounded us growing up, which kinds of lights have touched our soul. Our light affects us. The light we have not received is light we will receive when we do our work and we will learn from those lights we have not received yet directly from the spirit. And then our body returns back to Grandmother Earth because we are Mother Earth ourselves. Our body is Mother Earth and the body returns to Grandmother Earth. Grandmother in the native language they would say.

And now the story of the old doctoring woman is travelling through light as she leaves the mountain and those of you who have been tape recording the story can listen to those tapes. Maybe some of you might want to get copies from brothers and sisters who recorded it. I was reminded yesterday when our sister Beth was leaving the house; she said, "You should try to do this earlier." Well, I am trying to, but there are all these giveaways. It reminds me of gatherings when my grandparents would say "When is the story telling going to start?"

"We only have seven things to do before the story telling starts."

It would already be midnight and the time the story telling starts it would be four o'clock in the morning

Nee hinguth ka lee wa eetsch staewaten ta kanow a ten

Reminding me of the story told by our elders and how our elders would prepare themselves for this story by thinking about what kind of people would be there.

And if you are listening to this story you can say Eee Nae Weyth

Eee Nae Weyth

Neee neee que lee see en

Hay yon suen

Hum sta nee

Name of power. See en is name of doctoring power from Grandmother Earth.

Hay yon suen means you feel energy from the place you are going to travel to.

Hum sta nee means the power, any kind of power, feels your energy coming toward its home place.

The old doctoring woman is very beautiful
She decides it is time to travel in the light
And she leaves her body
She goes to sleep
But she leaves her body and her body
She tells her body to dream
But her soul will travel to the lights
Eee Nae Weyth
And she says to her soul
Eee Nae Weyth
She says to her soul, si.li
"Whee huns stee hut nee."

71

Name of first light she is traveling to.

Hut nee means the light of the relatives that knew us but died, traveling through their light.

My soul will become one mind with the mind of light

The universe

Eee Nae Weyth

And she travels

And there she is traveling

She is going to the sky world

Above the sky

Above the clouds

The bordering

Where the last sacred breath

The last breath of Mother Earth that circles the Earth.

Eee Nae Weyth

And this last breath of the Earth say,

"Oou nah nee te whoo

"Ha nee tee hetae hae."

These are names.

Oou nah is the name of the last circle of breath around the Earth. Nee te whoo is the name of the breath before the last breath that protects the Earth. A lot of people who became Christians thought that this was where purgatory was because it is a place a lot of souls go to and realize they cannot leave the Earth until they finish their work.

They go there and then return to Earth to finish their work.

Second line is a melody.

And the last breath says

Eee Nae Weyth

This is the last breath the soul has as it leaves this Earth

Eee Nae Weyth

And there she feels this breath and a memory

And this memory says,

"What ah net teth quan taelth."

Means looking down to the Earth; not just your eyes looking, but your

whole soul is looking at the Earth.
"Look down to Earth."
Eee Nae Weyth
And she looks down to the Earth
And she sees all the people
Different ones who are dying
Eee Nae Weyth
She sees them floating
Their souls floating out of their bodies
And they are looking down
Eee Nae Weyth
And it looks like their souls are like a giant eye
Their old souls is like a giant eye looking down
And that's what they experience
Looking down
Because their whole soul is like an eye
Eee Nae Weyth
And then the power says,
"Eeee na haieea yah ha nae lee na haleen etza sa wy neen."
Translated in the lines that follow.
Eee Nae Weyth
The power says to wear the clothes of these people
These eyes
As she puts these beautiful clothes on
This beautiful dress made of many eyes, souls
Eee Nae Weyth
And they live within her soul
And the power says
You will meet these people in their bodies
When you return to your body
Eee Nae Weyth
And the power sings another song
And the songs returning to her body
Aaee whoe ee ae ya hon nata na

Nae hone nae eee

One of her own spirit songs returning to her.

Eee Nae Weyth

And she returns to her body

And her eyes open

And she feels warmth all over her body

And she feels very different

She can feel these souls

But the eyes are really small within her body

They all seem to be centered in her heart

Eee Nae Weyth

And there she travels around on the Earth

She is called to go and doctor someone

To go and pray for someone

And it is an old man

Eee Nae Weyth

And she goes to this old man's house

The granddaughter greets her and says,

"Haek ka lee

"Whee stuts a han nah

"Whee see em ha

"Say hat stan son loth."

Translated in words that follow.

Eee Nae Weyth

She says, "Oh thank you for coming to see the old man

"He needs lots of help

"He cannot find part of his song

"Before he leaves

"He wants to sing his song before he leaves."

Eee Nae Weyth

And there she begins to sing

And she is wearing these clothes that is made out of these eyes

The souls of eyes

Eee Nae Weyth

Nee ya hon ha na ae
Hut ha nen na Doctoring song.
Hut ha nen means the warmth of the eyes from the back of my head are
warming the soul of this patient.
Eee Nae Weyth
And there he feels this warmth on the top of his head
And he begins to sing this beautiful song that she was singing
And he is leaving this body
And he tells his granddaughter,
"This is your song my dear child
"You sing this song when you are feeling sad
"Feeling alone
"And I will hear you on the other side of the universe
"And I will touch your heart and make you stronger
"And I will show you who feels the same way on the Earth
"And you will not feel alone anymore."
Eee Nae Weyth
And there he is free from the Earth
And this eye that belonged to him is free
But she has many eyes that she is carrying
And she wonders
"Do I have to stay on this Earth for a long time?
"Seems like there are hundreds of eyes that I am wearing."
Eee Nae Weyth
Whee nae lee
Hun say welth
Te slem en nea
Wee nae lee is the name of a place where the eyes never close, a place,
another dimension. Also doctoring people use this when a person is
depressed, to wake them up.
Hun sy welth is the name of a feeling, a place that tears people's souls
apart. Used by black shamans to tear people apart, but also used by
good shamans to tear a sickness apart, a place, the place it comes
from.

Te Siem en nea is a place, another dimension or another time. Use to put back together things that have been destroyed by men, their minds, aggression, violence; a place, a name of a place.

And there is a wind from the west

That hits her face

And a great cry hits her face

It is the spirit of death and it says,

"Wye eeee nee

"Helen yena Helen aeee

"Humma hylee

"Kaitens."

Wye eeee, is the name of a spirit of death that takes people by nature, like drowning, a tree falling on them, lightening, being hit by a rock. Helen yena, is a spirit of death that possesses another body. Other lost souls that possess someone and kills other people.

Helen aeee is a spirit of death that possesses someone so they will kill themselves so they will be free.

Humma hylee is a spirit of death that kills people in their sleep.

Gentle death, happy death, a person doesn't have to be sleeping they just go to sleep.

Kaitens is death of old age. Meaning the people who have finished their work on Earth. People started using the term old age when the westerners came. They never had such a word that invalidated people. It takes trained medicine people to learn these sounds. They should always be chanted with the story; not just outside of the story.

The eyes she is wearing are being described; how those people will die in this spirit of death chant.

Eee Nae Weyth

It says that there is a great death meeting the village

And the eyes that you are wearing are the ones that will be freed

Eee Nae Weyth

She did not understand what this was

And she could see into the future

And the eyes were showing her that the eyes she was wearing
   were the eyes of a future generation
They were the ones of the new people that were coming
And the great grandchildren would be ones that would be free
And they were doing their work before they come to the Earth
   because they knew they had a limited time
Eee Nae Weyth
And this kind of light was a light that had no time
This light was living in her body
It was a time from the past
A light from the past and the light of the present
Eee Nae Weyth
She felt this great sorrow on her face
And she felt so ancient
And she began to sing her song,
"Eeee na howa
"Ana tan na
"Eee na how na
"A hay ya a nae ya
"Ae less hun ness
"Ae hun nae."
Describing light.
Ana tan na means light that felt like a wind hitting your face.
Eee na how na is the feeling of light living inside.
A hay ya a hae ya is another expression of feeling, especially A hay ya,
   like living with the light. So you are being taught. That's why she
   was crying. She was so happy living with the light.
Eee Nae Weyth
And as she cried
These eyes they were very happy
And they sang to her and said
And they touched her and said,
"You will have great wealth for helping us many generations
   ahead

77

"Three generations ahead."
Eee Nae Weyth
And she could see diseased bodies
People were screaming
Very young people and old people
And there was a horrifying thought
A horrifying vision
Eee Nae Weyth
But they thanked her
And they said,
"Because of you, we were able to live a full life
"Three generations before our time."
Eee Nae Weyth
And with her life breathe she sang,
"Wha ha nalth tom nae oth mahalth naelth
"Neeth ta lae nooth."
Means condensed words of feelings in all the songs, in the twenty-two
songs, then the twenty third song.
Twenty-two songs later
The twenty third song she sang
She could see these eyes lifting off her soul
And then she is free
Eee Nae Weyth
And there she says to herself,
"Neth la ha na."
Translated in words below.
"I think I will stay away from the light above me
"And just will travel through the light that is on the Earth."
Eee Nae Weyth
She realized by always looking away from her body
And looking out to the universe at the lights
She was calling more work on herself
She was doing in her waking states
She was also doing work in other waking states

And the story says,
"An net te telth han nop telth."
"One hundred seventy-three waking states."
Eee Nae Weyth
And she said that was too much for her
That she'd rather just be simple
And be a poor human being
And wake up once in a while
Eee Nae Weyth
And there her sleepiness
Her tiredness was so happy
That she agreed with them
Eee Nae Weyth
Her sleeping spirits were so happy
That they were finally going to get to visit with their master
The beautiful old lady
Eee Nae Weyth
That the sleeping spirits were happy
And they said,
"You have finally come to your sense
"And realized that your light is just as important
"As the other one hundred seventy-three lights."
Eee Nae Weyth
And she did not question
She did not wonder any more
She knew there were more lights than that
Eee Nae Weyth
And there she went to sleep
She finally got to rest
And when she awakened, she awakened
In the Earth light
Eee Nae Weyth
And this light it said,
"Nee ooinga han nah aeil hainee thlenooe

**"When nen nae ya
"Oolea."**

*Names of different kinds of sleeping energies, different states of
consciousness; not really sleeping states. She mentions six different
levels of sleeping states that she is experiencing.*

Oolea is the melody.

Eee Nae Weyth

It said, "We will help you now travel in the Earth

"The roots, the veins of Mother Earth

"The lights that live within the Earth."

Eee Nae Weyth

And they took her to the Earth

The center of the Earth

This place that is called

**Wheelth ah na
Wheelth ah na
Wheelth ah nee
Wheelth ah nee**

First two lines mean the center of the Earth.

Second two lines mean the bottom or shadow of the center of the Earth.

Eee Nae Weyth

It's Mother Earth's heart

It's Mother Earth's life force

It's Mother Earth's circle

That lives in the center of the Earth

Eee Nae Weyth

And this is the all-knowing of Mother

The all-knowing of the Great Mother

Eee Nae Weyth

She travels there and there she sees a great river of light

Eee Nae Weyth

And there in the great river of light she sees her white canoe
again

Eee Nae Weyth

There she sees the white canoe
Heeee ya
Alay la lay loon no
Whe ya toun nae
Toun nae means the Earth center can touch your shadow, the dark part
  of your soul.
Second line is the melody.
Eee Nae Weyth
She says, "Where have you been all this time I have been
  travelling?
"How did you get way down here?"
Eee Nae Weyth
And the white canoe said,
"I always come down here
"This is where I regenerate from you."
Eee Nae Weyth
Even white canoes
Spiritual canoes that are all-knowing and -powerful have to be
  renewed, regenerated from human beings
Eee Nae Weyth
And she laughed and laughed
And the river laughed
The river of light laughed
Eee Nae Weyth
So much joy that was over flowing
Like joy was being poured on her
It was so much
Like a waterfall of joy
Eee Nae Weyth
Hun nee nan non
Means the light is laughing, coming out of you. You can feel the light
  coming out of you.
And she felt the light come out of this joy
This joy that had touched her heart and soul

And it said, "I am the light of not caring."

Eee Nae Weyth

"I am the light of all-knowing but not caring."

Eee Nae Weyth

"I am the light that knows the problems of people but doesn't care."

Eee Nae Weyth

"I am the all-knowing light that can touch people but doesn't care."

Eee Nae Weyth

"I am the light that knows how to help people but doesn't care."

Eee Nae Weyth

"I am the all-knowing light that will never ever care."

Eee Nae Weyth

And it laughed and laughed and laughed

And she wondered why this light touched her

The fire of this candlelight

And she looked at the light

And it was the light of the fire that lives in the longhouses

The houses of the people

The fire of this candle light

Eee Nae Weyth

That knows what to do but doesn't care

It needs the help of human beings to carry it

To use the light

And put the loving light and joy on people

But the light doesn't care

Eee Nae Weyth

That is your part of the work

To care as human beings

To do that part of the work

Eee Nae Weyth

And there she received this wonderful feeling

And she began to sing backwards

And the power song sang backwards
Eee Nae Weyth
The power said, "I can't stand it here any more
"There is too much joy."
Eee Nae Weyth
No wonder there are no human beings who live in the center of
    Mother Earth
Eee Nae Weyth
So, she sang her song going backwards
Going back into her body
Eee Nae Weyth
"Eeeee en na
"Ah na you hen
"Thung nae
"Hay yen yin."
Words sung backwards.
First line says my mouth is backwards.
Second line is my eyes are backwards.
Third line is my soul is backwards.
Fourth line is my heart is backwards.
Eee Nae Weyth
Singing all the words backwards
She sang backwards
Back into her body
When she entered her body again
And she started singing forward
Eee Nae Weyth
Whee he he oouya hae yah
Aee when na
Ae when na he
Means her whole life is going forward now. Turned around from going
    backwards.
And that's the song she sang forward as she awakened
Eee Nae Weyth

And there she looked around
And she was happy to be a human being
To know both the feelings of joy
And the feelings of sorrow
Eee Nae Weyth
And then Mother Earth, the light of Mother Earth said to her,
"Ooona
"Wee eee no
"Quee chil eee na
"Nawhost aye aye aye."
She was saying, the light of sorrow.
Eee Nae Weyth
And the light of Mother Earth said,
"Now I will take you to the light of sorrow."
Eee Nae Weyth
She traveled, she travelled through the trees
The light travels through the trees, the plants, the flowers
Eee Nae Weyth
And as she travelled, she heard many songs
Eee Nae Weyth
This is how those trees and plants would talk to her
Eee Nae Weyth
By singing to her in her language
Nae han nee
Whoo yo
Whee la
Hea na hea na
These are names of different kinds of plants that don't exist anymore.
Wheee la is something like kelp but larger, and it was blue, bluish
green.
Eee Nae Weyth
And the first cry that spoke to her was a light
And this light was the first cry of a child
Eee Nae Weyth

And this light told her this is the kind of light we use to put on a
person to remind themselves what it is like to be a child
Eee Nae Weyth
And this is the cry that draws the poisons of all the abuse and
hatred and terrible things that were put upon us
And it is absorbed into the tears
And this is how it comes out
The tears of light of the child
Eee Nae Weyth
And that power said to her,
"You will wear these clothes of this child."
Eee Nae Weyth
Eee yo whan whan na
Nan quan ton
Ten nae aye aye
Ton quon nae aye
Whan whan is the name of the first cry of the baby.
Nan quan ton is the cry the baby learns from an older person, from first
human contact, the mother.
Ten nae aye aye, cry a baby learns from the father.
Tan quon nae aye, cry a baby learn from both the mother and the father.
Other sounds, melodies are sounds she learned from cries of others she
had prayed for.
Eee Nae Weyth
And there the clothes she wore
It was like clothes over her stomach
And she wondered why she was only wearing clothes on her
stomach
The soul of these clothes of the child
Eee Nae Weyth
And when she returned back to her body
She got word from a young man that there was a lady who was
pregnant
Who needed help

Who had great pain in her stomach
Eee Nae Weyth
And so she travelled to the pregnant lady's home
And she sang the song she had heard from the child
Eee Nae Weyth
And the spirit returned to this child
The child it was the mother
Eee Nae Weyth
She was so lost
That even though she was pregnant with a child
She did not know why she was having a child
Eee Nae Weyth
And this cry filled her body
And she remembered who she was
And she shared that knowledge with the child she was carrying
And the child was happy and she was free
Eee Nae Weyth
She began to cry
And great pain come over her body
And that when she had her child
Eee Nae Weyth
The old doctoring woman who was very beautiful
She never, ever, thought she would see this kind of work
Eee Nae Weyth
And then she began to travel again
Back to her home
She sat at her table
And was eating smoked salmon
Eee Nae Weyth
Smoked salmon
And as she was eating this smoked salmon
A voice came to her
Out of this smoked salmon
Eee Nae Weyth

And this smoked salmon said,
"Ah na ha na
"Kae a way
"Eee ena huta
"Na hut a ena
"Sa kae lay."
First line is what the salmon is moaning as it is being swallowed.
Second line is saying the salmon is enjoying its journey down the
    throat.
The third line is saying the experience is enjoying the salmon.
The fourth line is saying the soul of the salmon is already in the
    stomach.
The fifth line says the soul is enjoying returning to the soul of the
    stomach.
Eee Nae Weyth
And it was light coming out of this smoked salmon
She thought it was the strangest thing
"I thought this salmon was dead
"Here I am chewing on this dried salmon
"And it is talking to me."
Eee Nae Weyth
And light was coming out of it
And the light said,
"We are the light that is left over after anything is dead."
Eee Nae Weyth
"We live for a number of days to finish our work
"We are another life that lives again before we leave this world."
Eee Nae Weyth
And it is called
Han nah net na tay maelta
Translated by words that follow.
This means, literally means
New life that is born from the last breath that is leaving this
    world

Eee Nae Weyth
And there she thought about this
And she wondered what the meaning of this was
Her feelings told her,
"This is why we sing
"Why we pray
"For the dead food that lays all over the table."
Eee Nae Weyth
Dead vegetables, dead salmon, dead elk, dead other things,
It is their children lying on the table, teachings
Eee Nae Weyth
And I guess that is why in the native language
They never had a word for death it is always changing
Always a new light
Eee Nae Weyth
And then this word is brought out
She chants this word,
"Hey ya hun na
"Hey ya hun na
"Hey ya hun na
"Hey ya hun na
"Hey ya hun na."
Hey ya hun na She is chanting which means I give my life up for
another life to live.
"I give my life up to another life to live
"I give my life up for another life to live."
Eee Nae Weyth
La hanae lae, la ha tess, ta ha nee
Translated in words that follow.
And there she looks at herself
And she sees different light living within her body
Eee Nae Weyth
And the light tells her,
"When you close your eyes

"There is never any real darkness
"There are just different shades
"Different levels of light."
Eee Nae Weyth
Ne hut teelth
Whees tunuth
Whee ee toolthses
First line means shades of light thinking of her,
Thinking of her in another shade of light.
Second line means thinking of her in sleep.
Third line means her thinking is thinking of the thinking of the
    lights.
Eee Nae Weyth
Nee eelee haea nae tethtiss
Nee eelee haea means the light traveling from all directions.
Nae tethliss means something to do with the many levels of light living
    in the mind of the universe.
And there she is thinking to herself,
"There is light
"Everything gives off light."
And she has the strangest thought in her mind
And the white canoe appears to her and the white canoe says,
"En ah wah nah too
"Suit spoo wah spoot na ha ee."
The first line means the ancestor lights of the poop.
Suit spoo wah means the poop reads our thoughts.
Spoot na ha ee is the poop tells the knowledge to other poops who live
    throughout Mother Earth.
Eee Nae Weyth
Even the shit that comes from the human beings gives off light
And there she has this vision of all the different piles of shit all
    through the forest land
From human beings, elk, deer, raccoon, mice,
Big to the little shit

Shit of all sizes

And she is looking at all these little bright lights through the
forest land

And it is the light of shit

Eee Nae Weyth

The final death of the person

The last shit that they take

They have light coming out of their hole

Eee Nae Weyth

And she sings a strange song,

"Whoo ee ahh na whoot ha mai ya

"Ha mai ya ham ah kah

"Wha naou."

Translated in lines that follow.

Eee Nae Weyth

She is chanting,

"Balls of light are coming out of your hole

"Balls of light are shooting out of my hole

"Balls of light are travelling through tunnels coming out of my
hole."

Eee Nae Weyth

Na hay kla han na

Tk la hay ah han na

Kt la lee sa nat ta na

Translated in lines that follow.

Eee Nae Weyth

And she realized that strong doctoring people

No matter how much shit was thrown at them

That they do not see the shit

The knowledge of that shit

They would see the light that is around the shit

Eee Nae Weyth

They never become weak

They become stronger

And she realizes why mistakes and problems can become
strength
Eee Nae Weyth
Kleee aye tee ya nee tee nee
The spirits of the wind take the souls out of the shit; that is why they
dry up.
Eee Nae Weyth
And the power of the wind
The light of the wind says that this is our work
And that we dry up the shit and we help it fly away
Eee Nae Weyth
To join the shit ancestors of the other world
Eee Nae Weyth
Nee la hee
Kleen na heee
Heen na heee
The first line means we are the shit ancestors.
The second two lines mean we are the shit ancestors that send the souls
of the shit to the Earth.
Eee Nae Weyth
And there she's so happy
She has a great smile on her face
Of the great knowledge she has received from this
Eee Nae Weyth
And she thinks to herself I am old and beautiful
And I know I will leave this world in a happy way
Eee Nae Weyth
Ka nae kan na nan than nen
Ka nae kan means my soul is traveling to this place.
Nan than nen means my soul is in the potlatch waiting for me.
And she begins to journey
To this place where she is invited
A gathering, a potlatch
Eee Nae Weyth

And there people are singing songs together
Gift giving People are giving gifts
Eee Nae Weyth
And as she arrives at this potlatch
She sees light coming out of the people
Eee Nae Weyth
She sees light coming out of people's eyes and ears
Eee Nae Weyth
And she notices some people
The light is very dim
That is coming out of their eyes
Eee Nae Weyth
And some people
The lights are very bright
That are coming out of their eyes
Eee Nae Weyth
She notices as people are singing for someone
All the light that is touching that one person's soul
From many, many people.
It is the prayers of their eyes and their ears and their mouths
Eee Nae Weyth
Neee lee hee hae can naou
We see people's lives when we are dancing in the light.
Eee Nae Weyth
And as she watches people dancing
She notices the people not dancing
Are touched by the light
Of that person who moving
The energy that is coming out of their body
Is entering the people who are not moving
Eee Nae Weyth
And there are people who are not moving
They are like doorways
To other kinds of light

Passing through this time to another time
Eeee ya nah lay
Tek ka nae wee ah nae
First line means the light of this Earth is the doorway for the Souls
  traveling.
The second line means the light of the sky world is a doorway for the
  souls passing through, by the Earth.
Eee Nae Weyth
And I'll stop there--finish the rest of it tomorrow

There are so many songs. I have a hard time trying to remember some of the songs. I have to pray really hard for these songs. I am really glad as I came here, I remembered; those songs were here waiting for me. It is such a wonderful blessing to know that if you forget these songs that these songs are waiting for you. Waiting for you to get there. That is the teaching of our older people.

FOURTH NIGHT

Nae hail cum set swet ten hut ten tu tel sut ten ken kawoon taehae

Translated in the lines that follow.

She traveled to the mountain

She traveled to different places

And we are getting to the last part of the story

Where she was traveling

And she was learning about the different kinds of light

And wearing the souls of lights upon her body

As she would travel

And she would travel in the white canoe

This white canoe was a spiritual canoe of knowledge, wisdom, of spirit

Eee Nae Weyth

Eeee Skonch

Ten nee aaeah

Hasee ya te

Tense stienn

Squalaelen na

Eeee skonch is the knowledge in the canoe.

Ten nee aaeah is knowledge singing from the canoe.

Hasee ya te says all the surroundings feel the knowledge because of the singing of the canoe.

Tense stienn means someone is feeling the singing knowledge.

Squalaelen na is the path, a road to receiving the knowledge.

Eee Nae Weyth

And the old woman as she was traveling

She was learning about the fire

About the element of fire

The light that we call the holy light now

Eee Nae Weyth

As she would walk the light would talk to her
There were many different kinds of lights
This light she had seen
There were blue lights,
Little tiny blue lights
And these lights would talk to her
And tell her,
"Nee ah kull sen quen nee
"Theils quiels nae
"Te quiels nae
"Te quiels na stiea ae."
Nee means to go forward, toward.
Ah kull sen quen nee is the name of blue lights, a lighter color blue,
    like sky blue.
Theils quiels nae means the songs of strength are touching you.
The line Te quiels na stiea ae means the songs are already with you.
Eee Nae Weyth
These blue lights were saying to her,
"We know you are walking towards our way
"We know you are walking towards our way."
And her power told her,
"We know we are walking that way."
Eee Nae Weyth
And she received the soul of these blue lights
She wore these clothes
She put these clothes on of the blue lights
And the blue lights said,
"See nay ya kense
"Eee nay yo kayo
"Flen neae aye a nee
"En nae."
Name of the different kinds of clothes that she is wearing.
First line, this kind of blue light is more of joy from elderly people,
    light that comes from them.

Second line speaks of blue light from adults.
Third line is blue light from children. En nae means the light is saying
    let's go.
Eee Nae Weyth
These blue lights are the eyes
The other kinds of eyes of Grandmother Ocean
This light that comes out of the ocean
Eee Nae Weyth
And she was wearing the soul of blue lights
She wondered what she was feeling
And there she was drawn to an old man's home
He was very, very ill in his body
Eee Nae Weyth
She travelled to visit him
They knew she was coming
A lady was waiting for her and she said,
"Eee ya hych
"Eee hych ka
"Siam ste whisch
"To na eee hee
"Eets kuts sena
"Nelth eee."
First line is from a woman, for an older woman.
Ste in third line means honorable feelings.
Eets kuts sena means you can feel the feelings of my grandfather.
Nelth eee means once we begin; first time meeting.
She said, "We have been waiting for you
"For the old grandfather is ailing in his heart, his mind
"He is waiting to leave the Earth
"But he can't until you come in
"And touch his heart and mind with what you have."
Eee Nae Weyth
This old doctoring woman who was very beautiful
She came in and she prayed

She sang her song and went around the house four times
And her song would turn counterclockwise in four circles in
    each corner
And then she sang again
And the songs went around the old man
And placed the clothes around him
That was part of his soul
Eee Nae Weyth
And he said, "Part of me was lost in the ocean
"Part of me was lost
"I could not find it
"When my wife died many years ago
"Part of me went with her in the ocean
"She had drowned
"But I knew I could not leave the Earth until it was returned to
    me
"And I knew that someone would find it."
And there he was free and his soul would begin to travel to the
    other world
Eee Nae Weyth
And the old doctoring woman said,
"This is how songs can touch a person
"This is how songs can touch a person's soul
"We must remember
"Sometimes we do not need to touch a person with our hands
"But we touch them with the soul."
Eee Nae Weyth
And she began to travel again
Nee questa quench ta
Ta mench ah nah quance
Ea a quals nun qye neth
Qual la wen ta na
Nee aa squal
Quan ta na

Translated in words that follow.
Eee Nae Weyth
Her power told her,
"There is another light coming
"Before we journey to the sacred breath
"The sacred breath that is coming."
And this light came to her
It was a light
It was a light that was very, very bright
Like this candle light
Eee Nae Weyth
And she put this on
These clothes
The clothes of light the color of this candlelight
She put it on her body
And she felt a great warmth
She felt a great warmth of love
Like the Creator pouring the healing spirit upon her
As she put these clothes on
Eee Nae Weyth
And she heard beautiful songs
From all directions
There were so many songs
And she asked her power,
"Talk to these clothes
"What are they?"
Eee Nae Weyth
Nee ah hunt stae nee
Te whets ka na si li si sili
Kae kanet tun sili
These words translate what follows.
Kae kanet tun sili is the soul of this whole expression, aura of the whole
  lights and people.
Eee Nae Weyth

And it said, "The soul is of the light
"The physical light
"The physical light for the people to see."
Eee Nae Weyth
And there was a great fire
All of a sudden around her
Fire all the way around her
A circle of fire
She wondered where this came from
Eee Nae Weyth
She began to sing a song
And as she sang her song the fire disappeared
And she could only see lights in the sky
Circle of lights
All through the sky
And she looked at these lights and the power said,
"Nee hat kana
"Yo wae kae kae yona."
First line means the lights are watching everything.
Second line means don't stare at the lights.
Eee Nae Weyth
The power said not to stare at these lights too long
For you will lose your balance
You must feed these lights from Mother Earth
Eee Nae Weyth
She had a vision
In this vision it was shown to her
To have a great feast for the lights she had seen
The lights are the same as these candles
Are the same lights we see at nighttime, the stars
Eee Nae Weyth
And this power told her
The Earth power told her,
"You must have a great feast to feed the people

"So, they will learn to be in balance

"When you talk about the stars

"You talk about the people

"And you feed the people

"So, they will not be drawn far away

"And they will not go crazy; out of their mind

"And they will not lose their souls by staring at the stars."

Eee Nae Weyth

So, this garment that she wore

That was these clothes made out of the souls of this light

They told her where to go

She was drawn to a very old lady who had lost part of her mind

She had been crazy

She never gave any feasts

She never fed anybody

She only thought of herself and the stars

Eee Nae Weyth

And there the old doctoring woman began to sing a song,

"Nee lia ae kaswena

"Kataes sta wan aee wa."

Kaswena literally means your body burns up from the stars.

Kataes sta wan means your mind and heart and soul will blow up
before your body, from the stars.

Eee Nae Weyth

There the clothes were put on this old lady who was lost

Her mind was returned to her

And there the old doctoring woman called the people together

Eee Nae Weyth

And a great long table that was on the ground

A beautiful table of all kinds of food was prepared for the people

Eee Nae Weyth

And there as they were eating, they became balanced

They became grounded

Then this lady who had lost herself before

She came to and she said,
"I know now I can share what I have felt and seen
"That I am in balance myself
"And how I can share while people are eating around the table."
Eee Nae Weyth
And as she shared, she sang beautiful songs
This is how she talked to the people
She sang what she had heard
She sang what she had felt
Eee Nae Weyth
And there when she was finished
She lay down She knew that was her last breath
And she knew that her work was done upon the Earth
Nee huts nee whenna
En noa ae wee lee suice
Hat to wit ha naa
Ham an not tee swiltch
Ten stele wee aee
Huts nee whenna is the last breath from the mind.
Wee lee suice is the last breath of my hearing.
Hat to with is the last breath of my feeling.
Ham an not tee swiltch is the last breath of my action, movement.
Ten stele wee aee is the last breath of receiving, like receiving from
*   souls of other people, acknowledging her own experience.*
Eee Nae Weyth
And there the old doctoring woman
She knew her work was done
And she travelled to many places
And she told the people,
"This is why we have the great fires in our longhouses
"The great gift that was sent from Si Sel Siam, the great Creator,
"To be grounded when we are talking about the spirit
"Or singing about the spirit."
Eee Nae Weyth

Eth thee will steeten
Translated in next line.
There she travelled and she could see the sacred breath coming
The sacred breath of the east
There was a great wind from the east coming
And these winds picked her up and covered her
And she could feel these clothes
Of the sacred breath of the east
Eee Nae Weyth
And the breath told her,
"Ah heee na oh no ya
"Han nat tah
"Han nat tah na taelth
"Oh whea ya."
Translated in lines that follow.
Eee Nae Weyth
It said, "The breath that comes from the east
"Is a great sacred breath that is given to us
"That is renewal
"That is new."
Eee Nae Weyth
"And this is the breath you will use when you are doctoring
"When you are praying for someone
"That you always pray for the new breath to enter the body
"When the mind is weak
"To ask the new breath to enter the mind."
Sut tet ka
Sut tet ka; s the breath of the mind.
Sta tee eelth
Translated in the next line.
"Then when someone is lonely
"You ask this breath to bring you into their hearts
"To strengthen their heart."
Eee Nae Weyth

"For each step they take upon the Earth is like the heart beat
"Each step they take is the sound of the heart beat."
Eee Nae Weyth
Eee nae a ta hon nah
E eat ta na tess kana ae
*Ta hon nah is life force from the Earth; like when you take a step; a life
force underneath your feet.*
*Ta na tess kana ae is life force of feeling. You can feel like you are living
in someone else's feeling, an ancestor walking there who walked
there before you; like on sacred ground.*
Eee Nae Weyth
And there she travelled
And there the north breath came, sacred breath
And it said,
"Ee len umcht tusch
"Yun licks teet quan sty."
Translated in words that follow.
Eee Nae Weyth
And the north breath said,
"We are the voice of the little ones
"The people of the north
"The little people of the north
"We are the ones that are always watching."
Eee Nae Weyth
"We are the ones that are always carrying the great knowledge."
Ethith quiel qualt sets
Qualtsen huts tet til quil tet
Ethlth queltee
Ethith quiel is a spirit that carries knowledge from the north.
Qualt sets is a spirit that carries knowledge from the northwest.
Quil tel is a spirit that carries knowledge from the north underworld.
Huts tet is a spirit that carries knowledge from the northeast.
Eee Nae Weyth
"Nee tee tee te telth

"Squaxin chalis steeeth
"Challum."
Translated in the words that follow.
Challum is the northern little people.
"That the knowledge is smaller
"We always pray this way with the north breath
"When someone's mind is weak
"We pray that small knowledge will enter them
"And will stay with them
"When you pray this way four times
"The knowledge will grow within the mind."
Eee Nae Weyth
"When someone is weak you pray with this breath
"The north breath
"And you say to the person
"That the breath is around you and grows around you."
Eee Nae Weyth
Hul en nae ken na na whees
Translated in words that follow.
This old doctoring woman
She found this breath to be too cold to wear
So as soon as she put the soul of the north breath clothes on
She took it off right away because it was really cold
Eee Nae Weyth
And she travelled to the west
And there
The west breath
She put those clothes on
The soul of the west sacred breath
And she felt many things
The breath said,
"Whe net whom cun huss
"Haes kae alam
"Na haim eee nae ta hat

"Tee nah nah hain."
Whe net whom cun is the breath from the darkness of the west.
Haes kae alam is the breath of sleep, those resting who are in the west.
Na haim is breath of the spirit that lives in the west and only comes out
at dusk, evening.
Tee nah nah is the breath of the west of early morning when she rises.
Eee Nae Weyth
This breath said,
"We are the breath of the ancestors
"This is where we live
"For this is our doorway, our window
"And when someone is losing their mind
"Or when someone is dying from aloneness
"Or someone is dying because they are still living with dead
relatives
"You will take this breath
"And you will say to the person four times
"Let this breath pull you forward
"Let this breath make you stronger."
Nae lay hums hata
Aae nael wel ha sal whet
Ae wael sen
Translated in words that follow.
Eee Nae Weyth
And she felt a great warmth on the bottom of her feet
And a great warmth on the top of her head
And on her side
But nothing on her front or the back
Eee Nae Weyth
She felt her body
There was no form when she could feel the breath
There was no such thing as form
There was no such thing as material or physical
Eee Nae Weyth

They call this spirit
Whae om hae halth whee nee La Scha
She did not like these clothes
She felt she'd better take these clothes off
So, she could feel her whole body
Eee Nae Weyth
And she did
And with this power she was able to pray for lost souls
She was able to pray for people who felt lonely
And she travelled to the south
And there the south wind came
The sacred breath of the south
And it spoke to her
Eee Nae Weyth
Being that she was an old doctoring woman but beautiful
The south sacred breath said,
"We are old, too
"And we will not let you wear us because you are old, too."
Eee Nae Weyth
So, they just became visions around her
All the way around her
And when she turned counter clockwise very slow
She saw pictures all the way around
And the south sacred breath told her,
"Eee nee ah
"Eee ya nah
"Whooae nae ta nae t sili
"Tems sha na haee aaee
"Aye aye."
Translated in words that follow.
And there they spoke to her
And they told her,
"We are the ones that carry the souls
"We are the ones that carry the heaviness

"We are the ones that carry all the emotions of the human beings, animals, the plants and the trees."

Eee Nae Weyth

"We are the ones that travel through the human beings

"And we take the energies that are negative, that are suptikten or knecht

"The ones that are ht,

"That are destructive

"And we send them through the trees, the rocks, the animals

"They work with them

"And they come back to the human beings and they become one."

Eee Nae Weyth

"We are the ones that travel through the forest lands

"We travel around the gatherers, the berry pickers, the hunters, the fishermen,

"We carry the knowledge

"We tell them where to go

"We travel around them not through them."

Whee ah nakue ten

Whee ah nakah teeth se wilth

Whis silth ha whilsh

Whee at ta tit

Whee ah nakue ten is the name of a place where a beautiful soul lives, but is very sad.

Whee ah nakah teeth is the name of a spirit that is beautiful, but very angry.

Se wilth is a place where the mind or soul lives that is happy.

Whis silth ha is the name of a spirit that is beautiful but with great sorrow, depression, never happy.

Whae at ta tit is the name of a beautiful soul of mind that has all these feelings, but like pets; a beautiful soul with all these feelings but not controlled by them.

And there the old doctoring woman

She thought,

"These clothes were so beautiful

"They were very beautiful

"She said it is too beautiful here

"Too bright for me to live here

"I must journey on."

Eee Nae Weyth

I am more comfortable with my old wrinkled body

She took herself away from this place

And returned back to the east sacred breath

Eee Nae Weyth

And there she went to sleep

And then in her sleep all the corners

The sacred breath of the corners spoke to her

And the sacred breath of the underworld

And the sacred breath throughout the universe

The sacred breath of all directions spoke to her

Eee Nae Weyth

All through singing

And she said it sounded like

Nee hay luk kan

Literally means millions and millions of angels singing to her, and also thinking with her; like being in a healing ceremony where you can feel many, many layers of prayer. People would use that word when everyone was working together. In our native language we don't call them angels, but call them lighted beings, lighted mystery.

Millions and millions of angels singing to her

Eee Nae Weyth

Whee shain ta ke

Literally means lighted beings that you are part of the altar and they are part of you; like standing on the altar. More like spiritually being one with them.

Eee Nae Weyth

And she awakened back into the human world

Back into the Earthly world
Back to herself
Eee Nae Weyth
She was very hungry
She knew she had travelled a long way
A long time through the elements
Even though she had feasted with the people of the elements the
    food is not the same as the human beings eat
Eee Nae Weyth
And she began to tell her family,
"Prepare me food now."
"Wha ha sun nee tuneith
"Ta hut ta sis
"Squanee
"Ha mai et."
What ha sun nee tunelth is all the salmon, food from the salmon.
Ta hut ta sis is salmon eggs.
Squanee is salmon head.
Ha mai et is smoked salmon.
Eee Nae Weyth
And she ate and she ate until she was so full, she couldn't eat
    any more
Eee Nae Weyth
And she told the people,
"This is why
"When we have visitors
"We must always feed them
"They might have travelled a long way."
Eee Nae Weyth
"We must never ask them,
"How are you?' at first
"Or, 'Hello, how are you doing?'
"Because they might be too hungry to tell you."
Eee Nae Weyth

And there the old doctoring woman
She was the one who knew all the taboos
All the rules
All the commandments of Mother Earth and the powers of nature
Eee Nae Weyth
As she travelled
The old doctoring woman that wore many clothes
She told the people,
"Ne han na la swetekat."
Translated in the words that follow.
"As human beings
"We wear all the clothes of the elements
"Every day and night."
Eee Nae Weyth
"In the dream world
"In the vision world
"In the spirit world
"We wear one at a time."
Eee Nae Weyth
"We wear one at a time
"Whatever kind of work we are to do on Earth
"If we are to work with the fire
"We learn about fire
"And we wear those clothes
"And it teaches us directly."
Eee Nae Weyth
And there she continued to travel
And she told the people,
"We are all of these elements
"We all have beautiful gifts
"We must take care and say, 'Thank you,' in all directions
"And say, 'Thank you,' to the great mystery
"The great Creator
"For giving us these simple gifts."

Eee Nae Weyth
"We do not decorate ourselves
"Because the powers have decorated themselves
"And they come and let us wear their clothes from time to time."
Eee Nae Weyth
And she made beautiful ceremonial clothes
Beautiful designs on the shawls
Mountain goat blanket shawls
Woven
Ah ken net ten
Ah ken net ten means anything made with mountain goat.
Mountain goat blanket woven
Woven what they called the second cloak beautiful colors
Many different kinds of birds
Feathers woven of many colors of the rainbow
Eee Nae Weyth
Ha lee en na
Keslee eeet nee
Kwalee nee eee
Singing about the many colors of the rainbow.
Eee Nae Weyth
And when this old doctoring woman was very beautiful
When she died
She said, "I will die four times
"Each time I bury my ceremonial clothes
"And when I die the fifth time, I will leave my human body
"Leaving my soul
"My soul leaving my human body."
Eee Nae Weyth
"Because my body will say, 'I agree to leave the soul.'
"And the soul will agree to leave my body."
Eee Nae Weyth
"And the mind will say, 'I don't know what to do.'
"And will remain on Earth

Eee Nae Weyth

"And this is why I will bury my feather cloak in the ground. Give
it back to Mother Earth."

Eee Nae Weyth

"I will bring my cedar bark cloak

"My cedar bark shawl that I wear

"Out to the ocean

"And give it to Grandmother Ocean."

Eee Nae Weyth

"Return the sorrow

"The tears of sorrow

"And the tears of laughter

"In the water you will hear me laugh

"And you will hear me cry when you go to the water."

Eee Nae Weyth

"And I will return my beautiful mountain goat shawl to the
mountains

"And I will bury it there

"I will have it buried in a cave."

Eee Nae Weyth

And there she said,

"My last beautiful dress

"My ceremonial dress that I wear on special occasions that has
all the beautiful designs woven into the dress

"It will be returned to the fire."

Tee hut kae te ha

Tee hut kae te ha means the ceremonial dress is feeding the fire.

Eee Nae Weyth

"To the holy fire

"To the holy light

"And all the brightness I carry

"And all the brightness that I felt for my friends and relatives
that I ate with

"That I visited

"All the ones I laughed with and cried and got mad at
"And they got mad at me
"It will be returned to the fire."
Eee Nae Weyth
And there she said,
"And the fifth time when my body leaves my soul
"And the soul leaves my body
"These songs that have been carried in my soul
"Will be returned to the universe
"The sacred breath that fills the universe."
Eee Nae Weyth
"That the universe is breathing in the Earth
"And breathing out to the universe."
Eee Nae Weyth

Quee ah nah

Quee ah tiss sleth la lamen

Quee ah nah means the universe is breathing in the Earth.

Quee ah tiss sleth la lamen means the Earth is breathing out to the universe.

And there she knew her work was done and she returned to the universe
Eee Nae Weyth
And the people remembered the old doctoring woman who wore many clothes
Eee Nae Weyth
And they spread a great table
And this great table was her white canoe
Eee Nae Weyth
And they put her body in the white canoe and they sent it out into the ocean
Eee Nae Weyth
And she told them,
"As long as the tide goes in and out
"You will never be hungry."

Eee Nae Weyth

And the people

They spread a table of the white canoe

A beautiful table

The table was all cattail mats

And cedar bark mats

Laid out on Mother Earth

And they covered it with pure mountain goat wool

And used that as the table cloth

And they had all kinds of foods of many kinds

Eee Nae Weyth

And the people feasted

And they cried

And they mourned the passing of the old doctoring woman

But they would get up and speak

And they would get up and tell one another,

"This is why we must learn to wear each other clothes

"We must learn to carry each other's feelings like the old
   doctoring woman."

Eee Nae Weyth

And the old people call this kind of work

This kind of medicine work

Whis kan na wan walth

Quee lee lee la

Whis kan na wan walth is the work of the white canoe.

Quee lee lee la is the work of the universe.

Eee Nae Weyth

They call it working together

Working together

Wearing each other's clothes

Eee Nae Weyth

Ee hain na kain na telth

*The work of the Earth. The feelings of the Earth. The feelings of the
   Earth are teaching us. Wisdom is the short way of saying it.*

And the great knowledge and wisdom of all the people was felt
at the table
And they shared with one another
And they remembered the passing of the old doctoring woman
who wore many clothes and was very beautiful
Eee Nae Weyth
Neeee thlee thlan nee ah
Nee thlee is the mind of the canoe.
Thlan nee ah means the mind of the canoe is my aura, my outer soul.
And that is all.
Eee Nae Weyth

That story comes from Lopez Island, originally the east side of
Lopez Island. The story was told by Wae Tess Ee La Ee Ah, the
old Wae Tess Ee Lah Ee Ah. The story came from our dear elder
Marian Cladoosby who lived here in Swinomish. It was also told

by a man named Spam Joe and another man named Joseph Bill-
-the old man Joseph Bill who lived in the 1920s who is Herbie
Bill's grandfather. And the story was also told by Addie and
Synopia and Synopia always told a long original version of it,
she loved this story so much. I am so grateful this story is shared
here in this gathering. The epic story telling is always a healing
ceremony. I am so grateful for these epic stories.

EE Hai Ch Ka

**MOON
BOOKS**

PAGANISM & SHAMANISM

What is Paganism? A religion, a spirituality, an alternative belief system, nature worship? You can find support for all these definitions (and many more) in dictionaries, encyclopaedias, and text books of religion, but subscribe to any one and the truth will evade you. Above all Paganism is a creative pursuit, an encounter with reality, an exploration of meaning and an expression of the soul. Druids, Heathens, Wiccans and others, all contribute their insights and literary riches to the Pagan tradition. Moon Books invites you to begin or to deepen your own encounter, right here, right now.

If you have enjoyed this book, why not tell other readers by posting a review on your preferred book site.

Recent bestsellers from Moon Books are:

Journey to the Dark Goddess
How to Return to Your Soul
Jane Meredith
Discover the powerful secrets of the Dark Goddess and
transform your depression, grief and pain into healing
and integration.
Paperback: 978-1-84694-677-6 ebook: 978-1-78099-223-5

Shamanic Reiki
Expanded Ways of Working with Universal Life Force Energy
Llyn Roberts, Robert Levy
Shamanism and Reiki are each powerful ways of healing; together,
their power multiplies. *Shamanic Reiki* introduces techniques to
help healers and Reiki practitioners tap ancient healing wisdom.
Paperback: 978-1-84694-037-8 ebook: 978-1-84694-650-9

Pagan Portals – The Awen Alone
Walking the Path of the Solitary Druid
Joanna van der Hoeven
An introductory guide for the solitary Druid, *The Awen Alone* will
accompany you as you explore, and seek out your own place
within the natural world.
Paperback: 978-1-78279-547-6 ebook: 978-1-78279-546-9

A Kitchen Witch's World of Magical Herbs & Plants
Rachel Patterson
A journey into the magical world of herbs and plants, filled with
magical uses, folklore, history and practical magic. By popular
writer, blogger and kitchen witch, Tansy Firedragon.
Paperback: 978-1-78279-621-3 ebook: 978-1-78279-620-6

Medicine for the Soul
The Complete Book of Shamanic Healing
Ross Heaven
All you will ever need to know about shamanic healing and how to
become your own shaman...
Paperback: 978-1-78099-419-2 ebook: 978-1-78099-420-8

Shaman Pathways – The Druid Shaman
Exploring the Celtic Otherworld
Danu Forest
A practical guide to Celtic shamanism with exercises and
techniques as well as traditional lore for exploring the Celtic
Otherworld.
Paperback: 978-1-78099-615-8 ebook: 978-1-78099-616-5

Traditional Witchcraft for the Woods and Forests
A Witch's Guide to the Woodland with Guided Meditations and
Pathworking
Mélusine Draco
A Witch's guide to walking alone in the woods, with guided
meditations and pathworking.
Paperback: 978-1-84694-803-9 ebook: 978-1-84694-804-6

Wild Earth, Wild Soul
A Manual for an Ecstatic Culture
Bill Pfeiffer
Imagine a nature-based culture so alive and so connected,
spreading like wildfire. This book is the first flame...
Paperback: 978-1-78099-187-0 ebook: 978-1-78099-188-7

Naming the Goddess

Trevor Greenfield

Naming the Goddess is written by over eighty adherents and scholars of Goddess and Goddess Spirituality.

Paperback: 978-1-78279-476-9 ebook: 978-1-78279-475-2

Shapeshifting into Higher Consciousness

Heal and Transform Yourself and Our World with Ancient Shamanic and Modern Methods

Llyn Roberts

Ancient and modern methods that you can use every day to transform yourself and make a positive difference in the world.

Paperback: 978-1-84694-843-5 ebook: 978-1-84694-844-2

Readers of ebooks can buy or view any of these bestsellers by clicking on the live link in the title. Most titles are published in paperback and as an ebook. Paperbacks are available in traditional bookshops. Both print and ebook formats are available online.

Find more titles and sign up to our readers' newsletter at
http://www.johnhuntpublishing.com/paganism
Follow us on Facebook at https://www.facebook.com/MoonBooks
and Twitter at https://twitter.com/MoonBooksJHP